REGIONAL ANALYSIS AND REGIONAL POLICY

Regional Analysis and Regional Policy

William H. Miernyk

West Virginia University

OG&H Oelgeschlager, Gunn & Hain, Publishers, Inc.
Cambridge, Massachusetts

International Standard Book Number: 0-89946-152-2 (cloth)
0-89946-153-0 (paper)

Library of Congress Catalog Card Number: 82-6419

Printed in West Germany

Library of Congress Cataloging in Publication Data

Miernyk, William H.
    Regional analysis and regional policy.

    Bibliography: p.
    Includes index.
    1. Regional economics. 2. Regional economics--
Simulation methods. 3. United States--Economic
policy.   I. Title.
HT392.M53   338.9   82-6419
ISBN 0-89946-152-2   AACR2
ISBN 0-89946-153-0 (pbk.)

Contents

List of Figures and Tables

Preface and Acknowledgments

This volume consists of three related parts. Part I includes two state-of-the-art essays. The first deals with interregional and multiregional input–output models, and the second is a review of the rapidly burgeoning literature on regional and interregional econometric models. Both essays presuppose some familiarity with the analytical methods discussed.

Part II consists of four short essays, which are updated and revised versions of papers presented to various conferences in this country and abroad. They deal with the evolution of regional development policy in the United States, and evaluations of specific programs. Two of them explore possible alternatives to present federal regional policies suggested by changes in regional economic structure and recent growth rates.

The last part deals with some basic issues in regional economics, and regional science; it is subtitled, appropriately I believe, "some unconventional views." The first chapter in this section, Chapter 7, attempts to integrate regional growth analysis with Georgescu-Roegen's new bioeconomics. The final chapter, which also deals with methodological issues, was originally presented as an address to the Southern Regional Science Association, and is reprinted here with only slight editing.

Parts of Chapter 3 are based on a paper presented to the International Symposium on the Ruhr Area, sponsored by the Konrad Adenauer Institute, Essen, Federal Republic of Germany, May 4, 1979. An earlier version of Chapter 4 was delivered to the Atlantic Economic Conference International Meeting, held at Salzburg and Vienna, May 10–18, 1978, and published in the *Atlantic Economic Journal*, Vol. 8, No. 3 (September 1979), pp. 15–24. I am grateful to John M. Virgo, Managing Editor of the *Journal*, for permission to use material from that article here.

Part of Chapter 5 is based on a paper presented to the Appalachian Conference on Balanced Growth and Economic Development, Charleston, West Virginia, October 27–30, 1977, sponsored by the Appalachian Regional Commission. Most of the chapter, however, is a revised version of a paper presented to the Annual Meeting, Western Regional Science Association, Newport Beach, California, February 22–25, 1981. I appreciate the helpful comments made by Lowden Wingo on an earlier draft of the latter paper. Chapter 6 is a considerably revised version of a paper presented to the Second Tokyo Environmental Conference, August 19–20, 1976. Chapter 7 was prepared for the First World Regional Science Congress, Cambridge, Massachusetts, June 11, 1980. I am grateful to Nicholas Georgescu-Roegen for helpful and incisive comments on an earlier draft. Some material not included in the original paper has been added to this chapter.

Chapter 8 first appeared in *The Review of Regional Studies*, Vol. 6, No. 1 (Spring 1976), pp. 1–10. I wish to express my thanks to James Hite, Editor of the *Review*, for permission to republish the article, with only minor editorial changes, and to Edward K. Smith, Patrick Mann, and Ming-jeng Hwang for helpful comments on an earlier version.

I am also grateful to The Rockefeller Foundation, Oxford University Press, and W. H. Freeman and Company, for permission to reproduce graphical material from their publications. Specific credits are given in the text.

Finally, it is a pleasure to express my gratitude to Lucinda A. Robinson, Dee E. Knifong, Anthony L. Loviscek, Jo Alice Evans, and Kathleen Higgins, for their research assistance on several chapters, as well as to Carla Uphold, Jean Gallaher, Sandra Woods, and Kathleen Minyon for typing the numerous drafts involved in getting this volume ready for publication. I also want to thank Karen R. Polenske for correcting a number of errors in an earlier draft, and for helpful comments on the entire manuscript. The customary caveat that I alone am responsible for any remaining errors or shortcomings applies.

PART I

Interregional and Multiregional Analysis: A State-of-the-Art Survey

Chapter 1

Interregional and Multiregional Input–Output Models

INTRODUCTION

A complete appraisal of input–output models would require a detailed examination of their specification, estimation, and applications. That is not the intent of the discussion of U.S. interregional and multiregional models in this chapter. Inevitably, when appraising any model, one must deal to some extent with its specification, or the theoretical basis for choosing particular functional forms. But the discussion of specification in this chapter will be held to the bare minimum needed to describe a model.[1] I also will largely eschew discussion of policy applications.[2] Thus the focus of this chapter is on the largely neglected problem of estimation, or the adequacy of the data used in existing interregional and multiregional input–output models. As a final caveat, no effort is made to evaluate fully all interregional or multiregional models that have input–output components. The input–output components of some "operational" models are derived from others. It is more important to concentrate on the basic models and, in the interest of brevity, to devote less space to models that are derivatives of others.

This chapter is a selective survey of the literature on interregional and multiregional input–output models. It includes references to books and articles available in 1981. It cannot, of course, cover work in progress—even that known to the author—except perhaps in the most summary way. Also, a survey can do little more than reflect the reactions of a single author to the published views of many others. The objective of this and the following chapter is to provide a concise overview for readers with a general interest in interregional and multiregional modeling. Those with a specialized interest will want to go to the original sources. Excellent general reviews will be found in Polenske [178] as well as in Adams and Glickman [2].

I make no apology for the data focus of this discussion. In the hierarchy of academic values, theorizing and model building are regarded far more highly than the mundane activities of number grubbing. But some highly complex models are now being used for making impact statements, and for other analytical purposes, despite the dubious nature of the regional data employed. In my view, if the data in any model aren't "reasonably" accurate, then no matter how sophisticated or theoretically sound its specification, the model shouldn't be used when important policy decisions have to be made.

THE ORIGINS OF INTERREGIONAL AND MULTIREGIONAL MODELS

Excellent, concise surveys of interregional models are given by Polenske [176, 178] and Bolton [19], parts of which are further summarized here. The theoretical underpinnings of interregional input–output models were first described by Isard [99] and Leontief [115]. Polenske has compared interregional and multiregional accounts in a 1980 study [178, pp. 44–50].

There is an important distinction between the Isard and Leontief models. Leontief developed a *balanced* model that is implemented by disaggregating a national model into its component regions. This is the type of model most often encountered in the literature, although its implementation presents a number of problems. Isard, on the other hand, called his a *pure* interregional model in which regional transactions tables are aggregated to obtain a table for a larger area. If the regions in a pure model encompass the nation, the resulting aggregate model will be a national input–output table. The data in a pure interregional model are gathered and processed at the *regional* level. To aggregate regional tables, data on interregional trade—as well as *intra*regional transactions—are required.[3]

The construction of a Leontief balanced model, according to Bolton [19, p. 4], has been called a "top-down" approach to implementation. A

second approach, he says, is "to estimate every endogenous national variable merely as the sum (or weighted average) of regional ones. National totals 'fall out,' as it were, at the very end of the process, and are not constrained in any way. This approach is called a 'bottom-up' approach. But none of the models I review is a pure bottom-up model, and I don't know of any operational model which is" [19, p. 5]. Three bottom-up models are identified below, but none is a multiregional model of the entire U.S. economy.

A pure interregional model was implemented for a large but sparsely populated region of the United States in the early 1960s (see Miernyk [144, 154]). This model consists of six survey-based subregional tables, one for each of the sub-basins of the Colorado River Basin. A pure model is now being implemented by Courbis and Vallet in France [40]. Another pure model, to be discussed later, was developed for Japan with 1960 data.

An early three-region model of the United States was constructed by Moses [163]. At the same time, Chenery [34] was constructing a two-region model for Italy. The Moses model (now generally known as the Chenery–Moses model) was of the balanced variety. He was quick to stress the inadequacy of his data; he also made clear the shortcomings of his assumption of stable trade coefficients. Moses regarded his model as illustrative rather than operational.

The first multiregional model that can be described as "operational," although in a limited way only, is the Leontief–Strout (LS) model [116]. The authors described it as "a rough and ready working tool capable of making effective use of the limited amount of factual information" available [116, p. 224].

An interesting innovation in the LS model is a set of "gravity" constants, $Q_{i.gh}$, in which i represents a specific good and g and h are regions. They are used to estimate interregional shipments, assuming these to be proportional to distance in the absence of factual data, from the "supply pool" (X_i) of a given region. If $Q_{i.gh}$ and $Q_{i.hg}$ are positive, $X_{i.gh}$ and $X_{i.hg}$ will also be positive; that is, good i will be shipped in both directions between regions g and h. The Leontief–Strout model permits identification of cross-hauling between regions, thus overcoming a major weakness of earlier models.[4]

Using Japanese data, Polenske [173] implemented a variant of the LS model. The Japanese Ministry of International Trade and Industry (MITI) had constructed a nine-region, ten-sector *pure* interregional model for 1960, and a later set of intraregional tables for 1963. Since both technical and trade coefficients were available for 1960, Polenske could use the LS model to estimate interregional flows and regional outputs. She then compared her estimates with the actual (1963) data.

The errors were relatively small for the machinery and construction sectors, as well as for "other" manufacturing and "all other" industries. But they were quite large in agriculture (up to 34 percent), mining (up to 59 percent), textiles (up to 62 percent), and chemicals and metals (up to 32 percent and 40 percent respectively).

Polenske subsequently developed an original multiregional input–output model (MRIO). Over a period of several years, she constructed an 86-industry, 51-region (50 states plus the District of Columbia) model of the U.S. economy, which has been used in a number of policy analyses, particularly in the areas of energy and transportation. Several versions of this model have been described in a paper by Polenske [174].[5] The definitive statement is given in her 1980 book [178], the capstone of a six-volume series describing her work and that of a number of associates.

The column-coefficient model, which Polenske chose to implement using U.S. data, consists of two sets of tables, one describing the regional technical relations, and the other the set of regional trade coefficients. The tables of technical coefficients cannot be used independently of the trade coefficients. The sums of rows and columns in the regional transactions tables are not equal, as in a conventional transactions table. The differences between them represent trade surpluses or deficits by sector.[6]

The most recent data used in the MRIO model are from the 1963 national I/O tables [178, p. 41].[7] Disaggregating the national coefficients to obtain state coefficients was a monumental statistical task. The most detailed explanations of the process are given in two books authored by Polenske, *State Estimates of Technology* [177] and *The U.S. Multiregional Input–Output Accounts and Model* [178]. State coefficients for commodity-producing sectors—agriculture, mining, and new construction—were calculated by weighting national technical coefficients by the quantity of commodities produced in each state. Since the Agricultural Research Service of the U.S. Department of Agriculture (USDA) collects commodity data in minute detail, the agricultural-sector coefficients are probably the best in the MRIO model. The mining coefficients in the national table are highly aggregated, and considerable commodity detail is available at the state level, so the mining coefficients in MRIO are probably quite reliable.

Manufacturing and service coefficients were estimated at the HERP using detailed output estimates developed by Jack Faucett Associates as weights. "SIC and input-output industry classifications [were] mapped into each other at the 152-industry level" [177, p. 30]. The following computational procedure was then applied to obtain the state coefficients:

$$\mathbf{a}^{n(1)}_{ij(152 \times 86)} \hat{\mathbf{x}}^{(51)}_{j(152 \times 51)} = \mathbf{x}^{(51)}_{ij(152 \times 86)} \Rightarrow \mathbf{x}^{(51)}_{ij(65 \times 86)} \hat{\mathbf{x}}^{-1(51)}_{(65 \times 65)} = \mathbf{a}^{r(51)}_{ij(65 \times 86)} \neq \mathbf{a}^{n(1)}_{ij(65 \times 86)}$$

where $\mathbf{a}^{n}_{ij}$ is the national matrix of technical coefficients for manufacturing and services; $\mathbf{x}_j$ is a diagonal matrix of state manufacturing and service *outputs;* $\mathbf{x}_{ij}$ is a matrix of manufacturing and service *purchases;* $\Rightarrow$ indicates aggregation, as shown; and $\mathbf{a}^{r}_{ij}$ are the matrices of regional coefficients sought. They differ from the national coefficients even at the same level of aggregation. The superscript numbers in parentheses indicate the number of matrices involved in each computation, while the subscripts in parentheses indicate the order of the respective matrices. "Hats" (^) represent diagonal matrices.[8]

The process of weighting by different state levels of output, sector by sector, guarantees that the regional coefficients will be different from the national coefficients even when the state and national matrices are of the same order. By reversing the process, however, the state coefficients can be summed to obtain the original national coefficients.

The one thing guaranteed by the MRIO approach is internal consistency. The question that remains is, Does this procedure actually account for differences in industry mixes and product mixes? Since I am skeptical about all mechanical methods of generating regional (or, for that matter, national) coefficients, I doubt very much that it does.

The algorithm used to compute MRIO technical coefficients in manufacturing and services is similar, in a logical sense, to the biproportional, or RAS method. The RAS method can be tested if two or more input–output tables are available for the same national or regional economy. A number of such tests have been performed, and these demonstrate convincingly that RAS is *not* capable of generating technical coefficients within acceptable error limits.[9]

The aggregate output of a given sector clearly reflects the size of that sector, but it tells us nothing about its composition. Unless one assumes an isomorphic relationship between size and composition of sectoral output, I fail to see how the procedure described above adjusts for industry mix. Clearly, it does nothing about product mix. But asking for that might be asking for completely unattainable perfection.

Trade coefficients were calculated only for those sectors which report interstate shipments of products. Thus 61 commodity trade matrices were constructed for the 44 regions for which transportation data were available. The 51 original regions were aggregated to 44 in the final version of the model. In some of the published results of MRIO analyses, there has been even further aggregation.

An important feature of Polenske's technical coefficients, in the column-coefficient version of her model, is that they show "regional" inputs regardless of the origin of those inputs. In her energy-transportation study, for example, technical coefficients are given for 18 sectors in the nine census regions. The coefficients for Sector 18 (electricity, gas, water, and sanitary services), for example, show the quantities of coal purchased per dollar of output by Sector 18 in each region. But one would have to go to the coal trade–coefficient table to find out which regions are shipping coal to each of the census regions.

In independently derived, survey-based regional tables, technical coefficients show *intra*regional inputs per dollar of output. Imported inputs are treated as part of *primary* inputs. One could argue that Polenske's a_{ij}'s come closer to describing true "technical" coefficients than those in regional tables, that they describe true regional production functions more accurately. However true that might be, MRIO coefficients do not accurately describe *regional inputs*, and therefore cannot be used for calculating purely *regional impacts* of exogenous changes at either the regional or national level.

The MRIO model has been used extensively, not only by Polenske but by several federal and state agencies, as well as by a number of consulting firms. Polenske [176] emphasizes that one of the strong features of the MRIO model is its internal consistency; regional totals must sum to the national total. If they don't, there is an error in the system. This, of course, has to be true of any error-free *disaggregated* model. But if there are significant errors in the disaggregated data, and if the model is used to make calculations on a regional-industry basis, the internal consistency feature of the model will be of little comfort. All these errors would, of course, be automatically eliminated as the regional data are summed to obtain the original national table. Unfortunately, there is literally no way to compare Polenske's disaggregated data with, say, survey-based data for a particular region. This is because of the conceptual differences between her "regional" technical coefficients and the relatively few sets of input coefficients in "stand-alone" regional tables based on survey data.

It is possible to make rough comparisons of total gross outputs derived from MRIO with the outputs given by a survey-based state table. This was done using both the West Virginia 1965 table [157] and Rodgers's 1963 output estimates for West Virginia [193]. Two-way aggregation was required since the West Virginia table gives more detail on coal production than the national table but less detail in other sectors. Comparisons could be made for only 18 roughly comparable sectors (the U.S. table had 82 sectors; the West Virginia table has 48). Rodgers's 1963 estimates were adjusted to 1965 prices. Relative differences between the two sets of output estimates ranged from + 98.3 percent to − 69.2 percent.[10] There was, in brief, little correspon-

dence between them. *A priori,* one would expect Rodgers's 1963 estimates to be consistently smaller than the 1965 West Virginia estimates. In exactly half the cases, however, they were larger, and in
some cases the relative differences were quite large.

Similar (and equally rough) comparisons were made between Sheppach's [200] estimates of 1970 gross state product (final demands), and
projected estimates derived from the West Virginia model. Relative
differences, measured as in note 11, ranged from +380 percent to
−99.2 percent. In some other cases, where two-way aggregation was
involved, the process of aggregation might have reduced relative
differences via elimination of compensating errors. It is difficult to
exaggerate the crudeness of the comparisons, but the two sets of tables
involved in these comparisons bear only the faintest resemblance to
one another.

It is important to emphasize that this is not a criticism of the
specification of Polenske's MRIO model. It is an excellent conception
that eliminates the need for the gravity component of the Leontief–
Strout model. The weakness of the MRIO model, in my view, is its use
of imperfectly disaggregated national data. The wide range of differences between estimates derived from a survey-based state table, and
state estimates derived from the MRIO model, reinforce the point
made in note 6. State MRIO estimates are part of an interdependent
national *system* and should not be used on a "stand-alone" basis, at
least not without major adjustment.

Each of the 51 regional economies is very "open" when compared
with the national economy. We know next to nothing about the flows of
goods, services, and final transactions among them. In the MRIO
model, trade flows were assembled "only for products that use the
normal modes of freight transportation and that are included in the
transportation statistics" [174, p. 176].

A persistent lament among regional economists and regional scientists is the absence of comprehensive, detailed, and reliable data on
interstate shipments of goods and interstate transfers of services.
Rodgers [192] has described in some detail the methods he used to
estimate trade flows for the MRIO model; a concise summary will be
found in Polenske [178, pp. 189–207]. Rodgers used a variety of data
sources [192, p. 17], but he points out candidly the gaps and limitations
in some of them. The detailed flow estimates are given in a 371-page
appendix table. These are no doubt the best estimates of 1963 commodity flows available, but they must be regarded as estimates with
unknown margins of error.

Even if by some chance accurate data on trade flows were available
for a given year, the MRIO assumption of stable trade coefficients is

not supported by the available evidence. A study by Emerson [55] shows that empirical trade coefficients calculated for Kansas were highly variable even in the short run. This corroborates earlier evidence provided by Beyers [17] and by Riefler and Tiebout [190].

Polenske has been cautious in her own applications of MRIO to energy and transportation problems. The difficulty with scholarly restraint is that it generally results in restrained analytical conclusions. In her recent study of interactions between energy and transportation, she analyzes the effects of *hypothetical* changes in trade flows [175]. A casual examination of Table 21–10 (p. 453) suggests some rather startling trade flows for coal, e.g., from the Mountain States to New England and the Middle Atlantic region. But an earlier footnote (p. 449) reveals that these are not changes that actually occurred between 1970 and 1973; they are merely hypothetical.

Since the MRIO tables are readily available, however, there is the possibility that other analysts will not exercise similar restraint. Once massive tables become frozen in print, they may be used without regard to the dubious nature of the data they portray. Indeed, there is evidence that this has happened with the data sets that have been assembled by the MRIO project.

APPLICATIONS OF MRIO BY THE INSTITUTE FOR RESEARCH ON POVERTY

One of the major users of MRIO data has been the Institute for Research on Poverty (IRP) at the University of Wisconsin, Madison. Several highly imaginative models have been constructed at the IRP using MRIO as one component (Danziger and Haveman [46]; Golladay and Haveman [80, 81]; Haveman [90, 92]).

Both the trade- and technical-coefficients tables of MRIO were aggregated to 23-order matrices for the IRP model, which was designed to investigate such income-transfer programs as negative income taxes and family assistance. The details of the IRP model are not relevant to the present discussion, but the central role played by MRIO is. MRIO data were used to regionalize the aggregate data employed in this study with only two modifications: (1) consumer expenditure and input–output categories had to be aligned (see Polenske [179, pp. 178–194]), and (2) small expenditure categories were eliminated with those expenditures being absorbed by larger categories (see Golladay and Haveman [80, pp. 147–155]). The IRP model is not a distinctive regional model; its regional components are based entirely on the

MRIO model. When the model is used to estimate and evaluate regional impacts of various policies, therefore, it is totally dependent on the theoretical and empirical validity of MRIO.

REGIONAL IMPACT ANALYSIS BY LEONTIEF ET AL.

An important study by Leontief and several associates [120] published in 1965 should be mentioned at this point, although it cannot accurately be called a multiregional or interregional model in the same sense as MRIO. This study was concerned with the industrial and regional impacts of a *compensated* cut in defense spending. The input–output component is a national matrix of input coefficients partitioned to distinguish between "national" and "local" industries. The model uses two "A" matrices, one excluding and one including households as an endogenous sector. The rather complex computational procedures [120, pp. 220–221] are designed to yield "before" and "after" effects of a compensated cut in defense spending.

This approach does not require separate regional matrices. The outputs of national and local industries, excluding households, are distributed to household and nonhousehold final demand, with the latter divided into civilian and military components. New levels of output are then calculated that include households as an endogenous sector. The regional outputs of national and local industries are estimated separately. These are combined to obtain output and employment levels for each region before and after the shift in spending from defense to nondefense activities.

The percentage distributions of the outputs of 41 national sectors across the 19 regions defined by Leontief and his associates are estimated from the following regional data: (1) cash receipts from farm marketing for livestock and other agricultural production; (2) an index based on value of catch and the volume of raw timber cut for forestry and fisheries; (3) wages and salaries of employees for agricultural services, and for the 35 manufacturing sectors; and (4) payrolls for research and development. Sixteen local sectors, for which local final demands were estimated, were included in the model.

Given a vector of changes in final demand (some positive and some negative, in the compensating case), a new solution vector of total output is calculated, as described above, and the distribution factors are applied to show the impacts on each industry in each region.

Operationally, this is a far less complicated model than MRIO. It does not require the latter's regional tables of input and trade coefficients. It is more restricted in its application, however. If this method were to be applied to a set of regions other than those defined by Leontief and his associates [120, pp. 235–236], new distribution factors would have to be calculated. Alternatively, one could extend the number of regions to 51 by using the same data to disaggregate the multistate regions in the Leontief model. For reasons to be discussed more fully in a later section, however, this method of estimating state output by region or by state leaves much to be desired. As in the case of MRIO, the logical structure of the Leontief impact model is not open to challenge. One can have serious reservations, however, about the accuracy of the regional estimates of industry output used in the study.

IDIOM: AN INTERINDUSTRY, NATIONAL REGIONAL POLICY EVALUATION MODEL

Like the IRP model, IDIOM is not a new interindustry, inter-regional model. It is a modification, and in some ways a generalization, of the Leontief impact model. There is a *national* model described by Dresch and Goldberg [52] as a "simple regression multiplier model," whose solution is the basis of the regional model. The regional model distinguishes between national industries (serving national markets) and local industries that serve local markets. Identical production processes among regions are assumed.

As with Leontief's impact model, IDIOM works best when applied to a national *compensating* policy. The chosen compensating criterion might be, for example, no change in national employment. The model allows for substantial changes in employment in a given region—or in a few regions—with national employment held constant.

There is more disaggregation in IDIOM than in the Leontief impact model (to 50 states and the District of Columbia). There is also more disaggregation of final demand, to nine separate vectors. The published results of some analyses have been shown for all states (and the District of Columbia), but others have been aggregated to 13 regions (Dresch and Goldberg [52]; Dresch and Updegrove [53]).

Bolton has given IDIOM fairly high marks, saying that it is "a major improvement over some other input-output models" [19, p. 264]. But all the advantages of the regional component of IDIOM apply equally to the Leontief impact model, of which it is a lineal descendant. Bolton also lists its disadvantages: "Like any input-output model, it is a comparative static model, capable only of comparing one equilibrium position with another...."[11] Its most significant weakness, he believes, is that it totally neglects the supply side. This is a serious weakness, particularly in view of the increasing effects that supply constraints have had on the growth rates of industrialized nations. It is one, however, as Bolton points out, that appears to be endemic among econometric models of whatever variety.[12]

Some of the weaknesses of IDIOM have been discussed by Dresch in the Adams–Glickman volume [2, pp. 161–165]. In his view, the most serious is that "sectoral technologies (I–O relationships) are invariant across relations" [2, p. 163]. He also notes that "regional distortions resulting from the assumption of common sectoral technologies across regions are exacerbated by the failure to take into account patterns of interregional trade. . . ." The model is thus unable to distribute national impacts accurately to states or regions.

THE INFORUM MODEL AND ITS REGIONAL DERIVATIVES

INFORUM is a dynamic forecasting model that includes a 185-sector input–output component. The model was constructed under the direction of Clopper Almon at the University of Maryland [4]. It evolved from a somewhat simpler, and more specifically input–ouput, model developed by Almon more than a decade ago [3]. The present model combines a conventional national econometric model with a large-scale input–output model in which coefficients are kept as current as the availability of new data permits. Some of the applications of the model to current economic problems are described in a short paper by Buckler and others [27]. The relevance of INFORUM to the present discussion is that it provides the interindustry component of three major models: Olsen's MULTIREGION [168], a second model that has gone through a number of revisions constructed by Curtis Harris [87, 89] (cf. Bolton [19, pp. 271–273]), and the Chase Econometrics Model for states and SMSAs [19, pp. 277–279].

Most of the report on MULTIREGION by Olsen et al. [168, pp. 5–17] is concerned with the projection of employment in 37 industrial categories located in 173 BEAs (Bureau of Economic Analysis areas). One can add relatively little to Bolton's excellent appraisal of MULTIRE-GION except to point out that the device used by the authors to "regionalize" national employment data is the familiar Location Quotient, about which more will be said in a later section.

MULTIREGION is designed to project changes in employment, population, and migration in each of the 173 BEAs at five-year intervals. It will be remarkable if it can do this with any degree of accuracy since the stability of regional variables is inversely related to size. The location of a new economic facility (or liquidation of an old one) can have a major impact on population, employment, and migration in many BEAs. The impact on the state or states in which a specific BEA is located will be much smaller, while at the national level the impact could be scarcely a noticeable ripple.

A second model "driven" by INFORUM was developed by Harris. Bolton cannot be charged with exaggeration when he says that "the detail of the Harris model is awesome" [19, p. 271]. One version attempts to translate changes in employment and output at the national level into industry impacts for each of 3,111 counties. The other version attempts to do the same for the 173 BEAs. Output and employment are projected (or simulated) for 99 sectors.

There is no need to repeat or to elaborate on Bolton's excellent summary of the Harris model. I am even more skeptical than Bolton appears to be (p. 274) about Harris's ability to overcome some of the data deficiencies that critics of the earlier model have pointed out. Finally, even if one could assume that the requisite data are available at the county and BEA levels, the question remains: How stable are the critical parameters?

The comment made above about the effects of a major change in a BEA on the reliability of MULTIREGION's projections apply also to Harris's BEA model. They are even more applicable to the county version of the Harris model. Both Olsen and Harris recognize this and attempt to avoid implausible results by imposing constraints on the size of annual changes in either direction (cf. Bolton [19, p. 274]). This is an arbitrary technique for keeping the solutions of a projection or simulation within "reasonable" bounds that can be defended only on pragmatic grounds. There is no theoretical justification for imposing such arbitrary constraints.

NATIONAL AND REGIONAL
ENERGY MODELS

There has been a virtual explosion of econometric energy models since the early 1970s. Many are linked to interindustry models, but not all have a regional component. Some of these are described briefly and are evaluated in Bozdogan et al. [25, pp. 7-12–7-24]. There is also an excellent survey by Hughes [98], who reviewed ten models. His article includes a table that summarizes the principal features of each. The first well-known energy model, hastily constructed by staff members and consultants to the Federal Energy Administration (now the Department of Energy), was the Project Independence Evaluation System (PIES). It has gone through several versions, and may still be in the process of revision. Among other things, the original PIES model developed a set of regional supply schedules for selected energy sources (e.g., coal) and used a linear-programming approach to integrate a number of other submodels—including demand models—to obtain projected equilibrium solutions. As Bozdogan and his associates [25] emphasize, however, PIES is a forecasting rather than an optimizing model.

The Department of Energy has also developed a Regional Earnings Impact System (REIS) to "estimate the growth in state earnings given different assumptions about energy [from PIES] and the national economy" [25, p. 7-18]. REIS uses the national input–output model to disaggregate output by industry and uses earnings data provided by the Bureau of Economic Analysis. The results are not fed back into PIES, however, and Bozdogan and his associates believe that "REIS is very inadequately linked to the energy sector" [25, p. 7-20].

The DOE has also worked with a second model, REPS (Regional Emissions Projection Systems), designed to measure the environmental impacts of alternative energy forecasts. National emissions data obtained from the Environmental Protection Agency are combined with regional economic projections made by the Water Resources Council. The latter projections are no longer considered reliable. But Bozdogan and his associates believe that if the model could project environmental impacts with reasonable accuracy, it would be useful not only to DOE but to private industrialists seeking new plant locations.

According to Hughes, "Regional energy modeling is in its infancy" [98, p. 102]. The major constraint is the lack of data. He feels that investment in a stronger regional energy and economic data base would have a high payoff, in terms of increasing the effectiveness of present energy models. It would also, one might add, help administrators formulate and monitor energy policies.

THE USE OF LOCATION QUOTIENTS TO "REGIONALIZE" NATIONAL INPUT COEFFICIENTS

A number of models use location quotients (LQs) as the principal technique for "disaggregating" national input coefficients to the regional level. The technique is so simple and easily computerized that one might ask what's wrong with it. There is nothing wrong with the

LQ as such. For many purposes it's an ideal analytical tool. It is particularly useful for showing differences in industrial structure—or conversely, the degree of specialization—among relatively small areas.

The major data gap in the United States for the construction of state or other small-area transactions tables is, of course, information about interindustry and interarea sales. If the origin and destination of all transactions were routinely reported to, say, the Bureau of the Census, the construction of state input and trade coefficients would become a routine matter.[13]

A modest step in this direction was taken when data were collected for the *1977 Census of Transportation*. As Isserman has noted, the published census "will provide shipments from state to state for total manufacturing and shipments for each state to the nine Census geographic divisions on the 2-digit and 3-digit level. However, at the latter levels intrastate shipments will be included with shipments to the rest of the region, so that exports will not be directly apparent" [102, p. 180].

"Unfortunately," Isserman points out, "funding has not been provided to code and use this treasure house of regional data to its fullest potential." If data on "imports and exports by originating and receiving industries would be processed and made available to the Bureau of the Census, development of regional and interregional input–output tables would be greatly facilitated" [102, p. 180].

Since interstate trade data are not available, analysts are forced to try to estimate the elements of production functions from such available data as industry employment, or—if available at the appropriate geographical level—income by industrial origin. The assumption is implicitly made that output is proportional to these variables.

One can test this assumption for commodity-producing industries. Data on the production and shipment of many commodities (e.g., coal) are collected and reported in some detail, as are employment data. Thus it is easy to see how close estimates of production derived from employment data come to the actual production figures. Such a comparison is made for coal mining in Kentucky and West Virginia in 1975, a year in which these states ranked as the two leaders in the industry in the nation. The formula for the LQ, and the actual 1975 LQs for Kentucky and West Virginia, are given in Table 1–1.

On the assumption given, one would conclude that West Virginia was by far the larger producer of coal. In fact, in that year, Kentucky produced 143.6 million short tons of coal, which was sold for almost $2.5 billion. Meanwhile, West Virginia produced only 109.3 million tons, but this smaller volume of coal was sold for more than $3.2 billion

Table 1–1. Coal Location Quotients, Kentucky and West Virginia, 1975

$$LQ = \frac{\dfrac{\text{State employment in coal}}{\text{Total state employment}}}{\dfrac{\text{National employment in coal}}{\text{Total national employment}}}$$

Kentucky	West Virginia

$$\frac{\dfrac{36{,}070}{1{,}064{,}000}}{\dfrac{189{,}880}{77{,}051{,}000}} = \frac{0.0339}{0.0025} = 13.56 \qquad \frac{\dfrac{54{,}210}{575{,}000}}{\dfrac{189{,}880}{77{,}051{,}000}} = \frac{0.0943}{0.0025} = 37.72$$

Source: Coal employment, [219, p. 401]; total employment, [213, p. 401].

[219, p. 401]. Clearly, the "coal" produced by these two states was anything but a homogeneous product. It is equally clear that the production functions in the coal sectors of the two states were widely different.

The differences are easily explained. Most of the coal produced in Kentucky is "steam coal," produced by capital-intensive surface-mine methods. Much of the coal produced in West Virginia was higher-valued metallurgical coal, and most of it was produced by relatively labor-intensive deep mines. The point is that if one can find such large differences in product mix and production methods for a commodity that is widely regarded as homogeneous, how large must some of the differences be when vastly different products are aggregated into "industries," particularly at the two-digit SIC level? The LQ, whatever its virtues for other purposes, cannot be used to estimate interindustry production relationships at the regional level from a combination of available national and regional data.

CONCLUSIONS

Little remains to be said to conclude this chapter. Interest in multiregional modeling has increased rapidly during the past decade, paralleling the growth of economic problems with significant spatial dimensions. Regional economists and regional scientists have stressed the supply side of economic issues more than conventional economists. And the supplies of energy and natural resources vary widely from region to region. This virtually guarantees that there will be even greater interest in interregional models in the future.

Bolton concludes his excellent survey by stating that "every model is useful in some way or other" [19, p. 287]. This is a generous assessment. He acknowledges that many serious problems remain, and doubts the wisdom of putting "many resources into multiregional models for small regions, certainly not counties" (p. 69). My own conclusion will no doubt be regarded by model builders as much less generous than Bolton's.

As I have suggested elsewhere [129], there is an impression that "operational" multiregional input–output models now exist. This isn't so if by "operational" one means that the model can trace the effects of exogenous changes in final demand—wherever they occur—to all sectors in all regions. If a multiregional model could do this, it could be used to produce all the standard multipliers of input–output analyses, as well as for simulation and other analytical purposes. The data requirements for such a model would be truly enormous. But if policy makers are serious about impact studies, and other forms of regional and multiregional analysis, they should adequately fund the agencies responsible for collecting the data needed to implement a fully operational, up-to-date, bottom-up multiregional input–output model.

If MRIO could become a true bottom-up model, for example, it would satisfy many analytical needs directly, at least at the state level. MRIO conjoined with econometric models could mark another step forward in the development of a versatile, multipurpose interregional model. As Jarvin Emerson has pointed out, in conversation (and no doubt somewhere in print), the Golden Age of adequate regional data is not likely to come soon. Until then, even "data perfectionists" must applaud and encourage efforts such as those made by the model builders whose work is described in this chapter.

NOTES

1. Further details on the specification of some of the models discussed here are given in Bolton [19], Bozdogan et al. [25], Hughes [98], and Polenske [176], as well as in the sources cited therein. An excellent summary description of a number of interregional and multiregional models is given by Polenske in [178, pp. 88–91]. See also her discussion of the modeling process on pp. 85–137.

2. This is the focus of Bolton's paper [19]. Some of the applications that Bolton does not cover are included in Bozdogan et al. [25], especially pp. 7–12 to 7–24, and in Hughes [98]. Both of the latter deal with energy policy issues.

3. Although desirable, it is not necessary to calculate a matrix of trade coefficients for each region; it is sufficient to have import rows and export columns for each region—

as well as a row and a column for trade with the rest of the world—to carry out the aggregation.

4. The term "cross-hauling" is generally associated with the practice of shipping *identical* products in both directions—a practice that is palpably inefficient and generally regarded as *prima facie* evidence of collusion. But it is important to distinguish between *real* cross-hauling and *apparent* cross-hauling, which results from the aggregation of unlike commodities over space, or the aggregation of identical commodities over time. The shipment of steel rails from g to h, with simultaneous shipments of steel containers from h to g, is an example of the former; shipping lettuce from Maine to Florida during the summer, and shipping the same product from Florida to Maine in December, is an example of the latter.

5. For a concise summary of the three basic models, see Polenske [174, p. 186].

6. Some analysts have tried to use the transactions and technical-coefficient tables for individual states on a "stand-alone" basis without, apparently, having taken the trouble to learn the basic characteristics of the model. It should be emphasized that Polenske has never suggested that the individual state tables could be used for strictly regional analyses. They are part of a multiregional system.

7. Some of the disaggregation was done by Polenske and her staff at the Harvard Economic Research Project (HERP), which is no longer in operation. Some was done by Jack Faucett Associates, Inc., a Washington consulting firm. The assembly of a set of MRIO data for 1977 was started in August 1981 by Jack Faucett Associates, Inc., under a contract with the U.S. Department of Health and Human Services (HHS). The new data set is scheduled for completion before the end of 1982.

8. A diagrammatic schema of this procedure is given in Polenske [177, p. 31]. A detailed discussion of the theoretical structure of MRIO is given in Polenske [178, pp. 110–137].

9. See Miernyk [150] and the references cited therein, especially Barker (1975) and Malizia and Bond (1974). Unfortunately, the MRIO algorithm cannot be tested in the same way.

10. Calculated by using $d = [(\text{Rodgers} - \text{WV})/\text{WV}] \times 100$. The extensive calculations were made by Charles Socher, a former graduate research assistant.

11. This is true of all interregional and multiregional models. There are, of course, dynamic *regional* models. For illustrations of the latter, see Emerson [55] and Miernyk et al. [157]. There are also dynamic national models, e.g., INFORUM (cf. Buckler et al. [27]).

12. For an exception, see Frank Giarratani, "Application of an Interindustry Supply Model to Energy Issues" [155].

13. The Bureau of Economic Analysis has proposed construction of a set of state income and product accounts which would include interstate trade linkages. On this, see Garnick's comments [2, especially pp. 31–32]. The chances that this proposal will be supported by the Office of Management and Budget, as of early 1982, are not good.

Chapter 2

Regional and Interregional Econometric Models

INTRODUCTION

The discussion of regional and interregional input–output models in the last chapter was selective. Most of it was devoted to the problems of implementing a few of the better-known models. This chapter is equally selective, in that it is concerned with a group of models published between 1967 and 1979. My objective was to maximize diversity; I hope that the sample is representative.

Relatively little was said in the last chapter about specification; instead, the emphasis was on methods of gathering and processing data. It is necessary to pay more attention to specification when discussing regional and interregional econometric models, although the primary emphasis again will be on the problems of estimation. This chapter does not touch on general theoretical or methodological issues even in a summary way. A selection of articles dealing with such issues is given by Dowling and Glahe [50].

The following discussion presupposes a rudimentary knowledge of econometric methods. One of the best elementary descriptions of a simplified macroeconometric model is given by Liebenberg, Hirsch, and Popkin [125], who describe in nontechnical language how a simple model of a national economy is specified. They also define some of the types of variables used in econometric models, and describe some of the steps involved in converting the model to a form that can be used to make forecasts. A more complete discussion of why and how a system of structural equations is solved to obtain a set of reduced-form equations, with elementary illustrations, is given by Kane [106, pp. 21–24]. Readers interested in a more advanced discussion, using the compact notation of matrix algebra, will find an excellent one in Johnston [103, pp. 350–357].[1]

REGIONAL AND NATIONAL
ECONOMETRIC MODELS

What is the difference between regional and national econometric models? In principle, the only difference is one of scale. Regional models deal with subnational areas, generally states or even parts of states. In practice, however, there are major differences. National econometric model builders are able to draw on an enormous data base, including reliable data on international shipments and financial transactions. A large national economy—such as that of the United States—is not very "open." Internal transactions are far more important than international transactions.

Regional economies, by contrast, are very open; even a large and highly diversified state economy, such as California's, is heavily dependent on trade with other states and the rest of the world. The smaller a state, and the more specialized its economy, the more open it becomes. The practical significance of this difference for econometric model builders is that the parameters estimated for national models tend to be much more stable than those estimated for regional models.

The most important difference between national and regional econometric models, however (and it is almost one of kind rather than simply one of degree), is the availability of reliable data. Those who build national econometric models can draw on an extensive—and steadily growing—national data base. Reliable state or substate data are available for only a limited number of critical variables. One of the most difficult tasks faced by regional econometricians is that of estimating regional data from national aggregates. The most critical deficiency of all is the absence of data on commodity movements and financial transactions among states. And the problem is even more critical at the substate level.

The lack of reliable regional data has been recognized as a handicap, but it has not been a deterrent to regional econometricians. An outstanding introduction to regional econometric model building, which combines a sophisticated approach with a lucid and cogent presentation is Glickman's survey, and his extended discussion of the Philadelphia econometric model [77]. Other excellent accounts of the construction of regional econometric models are given by Czamanski, in his description of the Nova Scotia model [43, pp. 281–353], and by L'Esperance, who constructed a model for the state of Ohio [121, pp. 81–119].

Three recent books on interregional and multiregional modeling should be consulted by anyone with a serious interest in the subject. Polenske's 1980 book, the last of a six-volume series describing the MRIO model discussed in the last chapter, includes an excellent survey of the general interregional and multiregional modeling literature and a capsule summary of 19 models in tabular form [178, pp. 85–137, 88–91].

Adams and Glickman's *Modeling the Multiregional Economic System* [2] includes 21 papers dealing with virtually every aspect of regional, interregional, and multiregional model building. It is the result of a state-of-the-art conference held at the University of Pennsylvania in June 1970. It is impossible to summarize the contents of these tightly written papers briefly. Suffice it to say that several papers describe the construction of specific models, whereas others deal with data issues and policy applications.

The third book is by the late W. L. L'Esperance [121]. Although much of it deals with the econometric model of Ohio constructed by L'Esperance and his associates, the volume goes far beyond that. There is an excellent discussion of the construction of state economic accounts (pp. 2–49). This is followed by a comprehensive discussion of various methods used to estimate gross state product (GSP), and a comparison of GSP for selected years calculated by various methods. There is also a chapter on policy applications of state econometric models. But the topic likely to be of greatest interest to analysts is L'Esperance's discussion of the conjoining of a state input–output model with a state econometric model (pp. 120–135).

A BRIEF HISTORICAL REVIEW

The first subnational econometric forecasting model, for the state of Massachusetts, was constructed by Frederick Bell, a regional economist at the Federal Reserve Bank of Boston [14]. Bell's was distinctly a pioneering effort. Not only was it the first regional econometric model constructed in the United States, but it was developed at a time when there were few national models to provide guidelines. It consists of 8 behavioral equations and 6 definitions or identities. These equations include 5 exogenous or predetermined variables (plus time), and 17 endogenous variables.

Econometrics is an amalgam of three distinct disciplines: statistics, economic theory, and mathematics. So an econometric model can be viewed as the statistical version of an economic theory that has been stated mathematically. The economic basis of most macroeconometric models is Keynesian theory. A regional econometric model, to be worthy of the name, also should be linked to some regional hypothesis or theory. Bell's model fits this bill; it is an econometric version of export-base theory. The weaknesses of this theory have been discussed in considerable detail by Glickman [77, pp. 15–36].[2] But when Bell was at work on his model, most of these weaknesses had not been discussed extensively in the regional literature.

Regional export income, in Bell's model, is a function of gross national product. Regional growth, in general, is assumed to depend almost entirely on national growth. Some of the more important variables were estimated from national data using the location coefficient approach. Some data, however, such as manufacturing capital stock, were obtained from an annual census conducted by the Massachusetts Department of Labor and Industries.

The model is basically recursive. Export and local service income were derived from GNP, and these, together with other exogenous variables, generated the demand for capital via the model's investment functions. The latter, in conjuction with a production function, yielded the demand for labor.

Bell "tested" his model by making "backcasts" from 1947 through 1960, with reasonably good fits. A number of variables—including real output, labor demand, labor supply, and migration—were projected from 1966 through 1980. The model projected annual out-migration ranging between 29,000 and 39,000 for each of the 15 years in the projection period. Real output was projected to increase 45 percent, while the demand for labor was to increase only 7 percent. The projected unemployment rate was held almost level, dropping from only 5.7 percent in 1966 to 5.5 percent in 1980.

The unemployment rate for 1979 (the latest available at the time of this writing) was, interestingly enough, exactly 5.5 percent, or the rate the model had projected. The projections of labor demand and supply— the only other forecasts that could be checked—fared less well. The supply projection was low by about 672,000 workers, or 19 percent. And the projection of labor demand was 501,000 lower than total nonagricultural employment, so it was low by at least 19 percent. One could hazard a guess that the projection of real output was low by at least as much as the labor demand or supply projections. It is clear that the Massachusetts economy enjoyed more robust growth during the projection period than it had during the period for which the model's parameters were estimated.

Another early model was constructed by Dutta and Su for Puerto Rico [54]. Larger than Bell's, it contains 35 equations including 12 identities. There are 34 endogenous, 15 exogenous, and 7 lagged endogenous variables. Unlike Bell's model, and other traditional macroeconometric models designed for forecasting, the Puerto Rico model was constructed to calculate export and import elasticities of demand.

The emphasis on trade is understandable in a model dealing with an island economy that is an integral part of a larger national economy. The authors state that the model could be "expanded to include additional relationships to explain price, wage rate, capital formation, and labour supply" [54, p. 331], but they made no attempt to do so.

A third variant was developed at about the same time by Moody and Puffer for the eight southernmost counties of California [161]. The authors experimented with a larger number of equations, but the final version of their model consisted of 13 behavioral and 5 definitional equations. The model was constructed to estimate the "demand component of Gross Regional Product" [161, p. 391]. The Moody–Puffer model fits into the export-base category. Ordinarily, export-base models are used to make forecasts, to estimate the impact on local, or "residentiary," activities of specified increases in exports. Moody and Puffer did not do this because their data on the components of GRP covered only a nine-year period. All they were able to do was compare the performance of their model with two "naive" "backcasts" of GRP components. It performed substantially better than either of the naive models (which consisted of one simple extrapolation, and one based on "no change" in basic parameters).

An early state model, designed for use in policy analysis, among other things, was constructed for Ohio by L'Esperance, Nestel, and Fromm [123]. The first step of this ambitious study was to construct estimates of gross state product. These estimates were used as the skeletal framework of a 27-equation state model. A unique feature of the Ohio model is its set of 7 "policy" or instrumental variables, which "can be subjected directly or indirectly to administrative control" (p. 798).

The Ohio model was used to investigate the implications of changes in prime military contract awards in Ohio, which evidently had experienced a decline in GSP as a share of GNP during part or all of the period covered by the model. The authors concluded that if the state had been able to maintain its share of the nation's prime military contracts, that decline would have been arrested.

The authors thought that for broad aggregates their estimates of endogenous variables were "adequate." But for some of the small components the model "estimated with much less precision" (p. 800). An appendix provided a useful comparison of their state model with others developed for California, Illinois, Massachusetts, and Michigan.

The first national–regional econometric model was constructed for Italy by Brown, diPalma, and Ferrara [26]. There have been "numerous empirical studies of the national economy on the one hand, and regional economies, on the other," they noted. "Yet, there has been little attempt to integrate the two bodies of studies, either for the purpose of explaining economic activity or for planning purposes" (p. 25). The geographic units in the Italian model are the nation's 20 administrative units. The model consists of four groups of equations: (1) resource-use, (2) production, (3) income and price determination, and (4) national equations.

The resource-use group includes five consumption functions (four private and one public); five investment functions; a set of net regional import functions; and single equations to estimate indirect taxes and "social contributions." A GRP identity is also included in this group. "Production" subsumes a sectoral GRP identity and five domestic product equations (agriculture, manufacturing, transportation, commerce, and housing).

The income and price determination block is the largest. In addition to a GRP identity (at market prices), there are five labor demand functions, two land demand functions, and a labor supply equation. There is a population identity, and additional sets of equations to estimate immigration, wage adjustments, land prices (quasi-rents), as well as the prices of consumption goods and regional prices. Finally, there is a set of six national equations, for which the relevant variables were summed over the 20 regions. All equations are specified, and 30 regional plus 6 national variables are defined.

The authors did not go beyond specification, however. They estimated neither parameters nor endogenous variables. The reason for including this study in a historical review is that it defines a new approach to regional econometric model building. The authors state, "Klein has developed an approach to regional model building which differs in one basic respect from that pursued here. He suggests linking a regional submodel to a national model (as one links industry models to a national model). In our approach, we are constructing a complete set of interrelated regional models within a national accounts framework" [26, p. 25].

A regional model, tied to the national economy, was developed for the Northeast Corridor by Crow [41].[3] This was the first U.S. regional model to be used in tandem with a national model, in the present case the Wharton Economic Forecasting Associates Quarterly Model.

The model was designed to be used for forecasting and simulation, with emphasis on the latter. It is fairly large, having 42 structural equations and 6 identities. There are 19 exogenous and 30 endogenous variables. The data consist of time-series observations from 1949 to 1963, expressed in current rather than constant dollars because of the absence of regional price data.

The model was tested by comparing actual with calculated variables. In most cases the fit was reasonably good. It was also used to simulate the impact of alternative military spending policies on the Northeast Corridor.

The details of the simulation were not given, but, as Crow concluded, "The regional simulation tracked the national results fairly closely and seemed to be quite reasonable, given the projected shares of military and non-military procurement in the three Corridor regions" [41, p. 203].[4]

The relationship between the national and regional economies was stated cogently by Adams, Brooking, and Glickman in their report on an econometric model constructed for the state of Mississippi. They described the regional economy as a "satellite" of the national economy:

> The regional model builder needs to predict the evolution of the regional economy in the national economic setting. Like the small country economist, he takes the external (national) environment as given. If the region is small and industrially diversified, the feedbacks between regional developments and the national outlook are likely also to be small. In this sense the regional model builder can structure his model as a satellite of the national economy, the causation running from national developments to the region but not from the region to the nation. [1, p. 286]

Adams, Brooking, and Glickman mention several other differences between national and regional models: (1) the final demand identity of the Keynesian model is replaced by gross state product, the sum of gross output by sector, and (2) some important demand relationships in national models are formulated explicitly, but are only implicit in regional models.

The Mississippi model consists of four blocks of equations: (1) output, (2) employment, (3) wage rates and personal income, and (4) a tax block. Together there are 39 structural equations and 86 endogenous variables (plus time). They were used to "backcast" gross state product from 1955 to 1970, with a remarkably close fit. The authors also projected GSP, employment and unemployment, personal income, per capita income, manufacturing and farm wage rates, and sales tax collections from 1972 to 1980. At the time of this writing, data were not available to check the accuracy of these forecasts.

A model designed to estimate the regional impact of monetary policy on Indiana was constructed by Fishkind [59]. It is a short-run, 34-equation model with 17 structural equations. It is recursive in a limited sense. Demand for the state's basic outputs is expressed as a function of strictly exogenous variables, gross national product, and the yield on corporate bonds (p. 82). An unusual feature of the Indiana model is that it includes three channels by which monetary policy can be transmitted to the state: the cost of capital; availability of capital; and "the wealth effect."

The Indiana model was used to simulate the impact of national monetary policy on Indiana during 1969–70 and 1971–72. The author found a "differential regional impact of monetary policy. Moreover, this differential impact appears to be asymmetrical. During periods of substantial growth the Indiana economy grows at much the same rate as the national economy. On the other hand, during periods of monetary restraint the Indiana economy grows much more slowly than the national economy" [59, p. 84]. An extremely useful feature of Fishkind's study is a tabular comparison of 12 regional econometric models, including some of those discussed in this chapter (pp. 86–87).

Ballard and Glickman developed an unusual multiregional forecasting model for the Delaware Valley [8].[5] Its distinguishing feature is that it is not linked to the national economy, as is the customary case. Instead, it was constructed to demonstrate "a pattern of trends within an area. There is no reference to influences from outlying areas, or to possible inconsistencies with the national forecasts" (p. 161).

The objective was to disaggregate the regional model into 12 subregions (in this case, counties and 3 SMSAs). The model is relatively small, consisting of 13 structural equations and 4 identities. It contains 44 endogenous and 19 exogenous variables, and the parameters were estimated from data covering a fairly long period—1950 through 1972. It was used to estimate differences in gross product, total employment, personal income, and population among counties. Measures of elasticity for each of these variables were also calculated for the counties, and for the entire region. Finally, the model was used to simulate the impact on each county of a hypothetical industrial park to be located in Chester and Delaware counties.

A recent model, which differs in a number of respects from those discussed thus far, was constructed by Latham, Lewis, and Landon for the state of Delaware [111]. The features that distinguish it from earlier efforts are: "(1) The region to be modeled is truly small, (2) the model is estimated with quarterly rather than annual data, (3) the basic accounting identity around which the model is constructed is gross regional income rather than gross regional product, and (4) the model introduces the use of a more elaborate microeconomic theory of the labor market into regional modeling" (p. 1).

Not only is Delaware small, but its economy is not highly diversified. Interindustry linkages are undoubtedly weak. As the authors point out: "In small regions single firms can have inordinately large impacts on the region's economy, (e.g., in Delaware one employer accounts for more than 13 percent of total employment in the state)" [111, p. 2].

The model comprises four endogenous blocks: (1) personal income, (2) the labor market (consisting of wage, man-hours, and employment equations, plus the wage bill and average hours identities for 18 industrial sectors), (3) the labor force, where the size of the work force and the number of unemployed are determined, and (4) state taxes divided into 14 categories.

A cursory examination suggests that the model forecasts employment, personal income, and state tax revenues reasonably well. But, as the authors point out, "The fact that model error exceeds total error in some cases may indicate that the forecasts are not quite as good as they appear to be at first because of fortuitous offsetting effects of exogenous and model errors" [111, p. 12].

Finally, the authors make the interesting observation that political and institutional difficulties are at least as formidable in a small state as econometric and conceptual problems. A large employer in such a state is almost certain to exert strong political influence, and because this employer can have an enormous impact on the state economy, fluctuations in income, output, and employment in that firm loom large in state aggregates. It is not surprising that the cooperation of state agencies "ranged from excellent to marginal" [111, p. 13]. This is the sort of problem that can be fully appreciated only by regional economists who have engaged in empirical research in areas where government agencies become almost subservient to a firm that dominates the area economy.

Regional econometric model bulding is a relatively new art, dating only from 1967, when Bell published his Massachusetts model. The most active, and one of the more imaginative, practitioners of the art has been Glickman, whose Philadelphia model is a landmark in regional econometric research. The original version of the Philadelphia model, published in 1971, is impressive [78]. Glickman continued to refine his model, however, and to expand its potential use. Others, particularly Hall and Licari [83], have contributed to the development and elaboration of the Glickman model.[6]

An interesting feature of the Philadelphia model is that it evolved through a number of stages. The first version was a three-sector, 26-equation, block-recursive model. In the next stage Glickman increased the number of industries and added equations to estimate demographic, local government, retail trade, and banking activities. The number of equations was increased to more than 100. In the third modification, "the concept of space in econometric models was extended" [77, p. 76]. The final version offers still more industrial and spatial disaggregation. This version, described in Glickman's 1977 book, consists of 228 equations, which include 30 exogenous national variables, 17 regional exogenous variables, and 44 lagged endogenous variables. The areal stratification distinguishes between the city of Philadelphia and its suburbs.

The enlarged model has retained its block simultaneous nature, and it follows what Glickman has called "a modified economic [export] base approach" [77, p. 78]. It was designed to be linked to the Wharton Annual and Industrial Forecasting Model so that "forecasts derived from the national model can be translated into regional forecasts" (p. 78).

Glickman's model was used for a variety of policy-analytic simulation experiments. These included estimates of the impacts of oil shortages, a public service employment program, revenue sharing, defense spending, and a balanced city budget on the region. It was also used to make long-run forecasts of a number of critical variables through 1982 [77, pp. 160–180].

MULTIREGIONAL ECONOMETRIC MODELS

Regional and multiregional econometric model building had come a long way by 1980. The May 1980 issue of the *Journal of Regional Science* included several papers presented to a symposium on multiregional forecasting and policy-simulation models. In addition to an editor's foreword by Benjamin Stevens and an introduction by Roger Bolton [18], there were papers by Ballard and Wendling [10], Harris [88], Milne, Glickman, and Adams [159], and Treyz [207].[7]

The papers dealing with specific models are summaries; they do not describe in detail all the problems of specification, estimation, and application. Analysts interested in adapting these models to their own uses would have to go to other sources—or to the authors—to learn about operational details, and the inevitable problems involved in application. But that doesn't diminish the usefulness of these papers for readers interested in an overview of new developments in spatial econometric model building; in fact, it enhances their usefulness.

These overviews of complex systems would have lost their effectiveness if the authors had attempted to go into operational detail.

Bolton's introduction [18] provides a lucid summary of the state of the art of multiregional model building as of 1980. His "model of a model" (p. 134) is as good a general description of multiregional models—and the regional models embedded in them—as one can find. It describes the blocks of equations that make up such models, and it shows the direction of causation of a typical "top-down" national-multiregional model. It also shows that the relationship between some blocks is simultaneous, while between others it is recursive.

The issue of "top-down" (TD) versus "bottom-up" (BU) construction of multiregional input–output models was discussed in the last chapter. But that discussion dealt only with aggregation versus disaggregation from a data-gathering or statistical point of view. In econometric model building, however, the TD–BU issue is theoretically as well as statistically significant.

The typical regional model is, explicitly or implicitly, an export-base model; regional output is a function of national demand for the goods and services a given region exports. This assumption underlies conventional multiregional econometric models as well. The national variables that determine the level and composition of regional economic activity are exogenous, as in the case of the "linked" models discussed in the last section (e.g., Glickman [77]). Similarly, in the conventional multiregional model, "national variables are predicted first, often by a completely isolated national model built by someone else, and then regional variables are determined as shares of the fixed total, in a 'top-down' approach" [18, p. 133].

In a bottom-up multiregional model, however, "many national variables are not exogenous to regions, but are dependent on the level and distribution of regional variables. The nation is *defined* as the sum—or average—of the regions, rather than being a fixed pie divided up among them. National variables are determined by summing up regions (as in employment) or by averaging (as in wage rates)" [18, p. 33]. The distinction is a significant one. It tells us, among other things, that the level and composition of regional economic activity are not *entirely* dependent on export demand; to some extent they may be the result of completely endogenous forces.

The National-Regional Impact Evaluation System (NRIES) described by Ballard and Wendling [10] differs from most regional or multiregional models in a number of respects.[8] It is, first, a bottom-up model: "The national model is derived simply as the sum of the 51 [50 states plus D.C.] independently-constructed state models. In each of the state models variable relationships are determined by econometric time-series estimation techniques. For each variable in each state, the model generated individual growth patterns as if there were 51 separate single-region econometric models. National growth trends *are thus determined* by regional growth and not vice versa" [10, p. 144, emphasis added].[9]

A second interesting characteristic of NRIES is that it includes explicit spatial variables called "interaction" variables. They are "distance deflated," which means they are gravity-type variables. As Ballard and Wendling put it, "while economic activity in California impacts the economies of both Connecticut and Nevada, the influence on Nevada is much greater" [10, p. 44].

A third important difference between NRIES and most multiregional models is that some of the system's equations are nonlinear. This imposes two constraints on the model. Nonlinearity precludes calculation of a reduced form, which would provide unique solutions for all variables. This, in turn, means that accuracy tests cannot be applied to the model as a whole; such tests are limited to individual variables [10, p. 150, and the references cited].[10]

Ballard and Wendling used the NRIES model to make two forecasts. The first, which they call a "baseline forecast," assumes no major change in the structure of state economies; the second estimates "the regional impacts of a national policy to reduce substantially the unemployment rate" [10, p. 153]. The goal hypothesized is a national unemployment rate of 4.5 percent in 1982. The policy variables changed to simulate the projected goal were government spending (increased) and personal income taxes (reduced).

The projected variables for each state (and the United States) were income, employment, per capita disposable income, state and local government revenues, and unemployment rates. The projections were positive for the first four variables, except for fractional declines in Alaska and South Dakota. The model projected declining unemployment rates in all states, except in North and South Dakota, where there was no change.

Large increases in income and employment, with correspondingly large declines in unemployment, were projected for Michigan and Ohio. The authors did not explain the substantial variation among states, nor the declines mentioned in the preceding paragraph. These projections must be regarded as simulations since the policy changes hypothesized are a far cry from those proposed during the days of the Carter administration (as well as those proposed by the Reagan administration).

Curtis Harris's Multi-Industry Forecasting Model (MRMI) is one of the oldest, if not the first, multiregional econometric model constructed

[88]. It deals with geographic areas smaller than those in other multiregional models. An early version was published in 1973, but there have been many modifications since then. Harris links his model to traditional (i.e., Weberian) location theory via a "location rent" equation. The existence of location rents (either profits or land rent), he assumes, will induce changes in location.

The model consists of a set of industry location equations. The independent variables are components of profits. Explanatory variables include marginal transportation costs, wage rates, land values, "prior investments in equipment, prior production and agglomeration variables" [88, p. 162]. Agglomeration forces are subsumed under population density, as well as "the economic size of major buyers, and the economic size of major suppliers" (p. 162).

A unique feature of Harris's model is the use of a linear programming algorithm to estimate transportation shadow prices. The latest version of MRMI is more aggregated than earlier formulations. A total demand variable has replaced separate estimates for major buyers in each region, and a single estimate of input scarcity has replaced earlier estimates for major suppliers.

Harris believes this has strengthened the theoretical basis of the model by shifting the focus from components of cost to profits. The use of fewer variables has minimized earlier problems engendered by multicollinearity. And the use of location rent in place of cost variables, he feels, has expanded the range of applications of the model. He does not make clear, however, why he thinks so.

The model is recursive. Industry output is projected for one period, then other variables are derived. The latter are used to project industry output for the next period, and so on. MRMI is tied to Almon's INFORUM [4], a well-known national interindustry forecasting model. All the equations in MRMI estimate regional shares. This top-down approach ensures consistency with the national projections.

Harris has collected data for 1,100 items for 3,111 "county-type" areas.[11] Many of the county variables are estimated from national data, and Harris concedes that the margin of error increases with spatial disaggregation.

Harris defends the use of counties as the appropriate unit for spatial analysis on the pragmatic ground that the county version of the model is the one most users request. He also argues, however, that theory dictates the use of small geographic areas since business and household location decisions are made on the basis of specific sites, not broad geographic regions.

The model has been used for a variety of purposes, including estimates of regional economic impacts of the national highway system, piggyback truck shipments, changes in gasoline prices, on-shore effects of off-shore oil wells, new coal mines, cutbacks in natural gas (in a specified area), and reduced agricultural production in a given region.

Statistical tests of the model's performance are not given. Harris states, however, that "using only 1965 and 1966 data, the model predicted certain changes in trends that have become apparent in the 1970's, such as the relative increase in growth in the South and the slowdown of growth in the Far West" [88, p. 170]. This statement tells us nothing, however, about the accuracy of the model's projections of small-area impacts. It would be interesting to see an evaluation of the reliability of the estimates of impacts mentioned in the preceding paragraph.

The Milne–Glickman–Adams (MGA) multiregional model of the United States is a regional disaggregation of the Wharton Annual and Industry Model [159]. Its authors defend their top-down approach with vigor:

> . . .National growth trends are allocated to regions based on their competitiveness and the structure of regional industry. The advantage of this method over the "bottom-up" approach. . .is that consistency is ensured in the regional projections. Furthermore, with the present state of regional data in the United States, one can have far more confidence in relationships developed at the national level than those developed at the regional level. [159, p. 175]

They go on to point out, however, that "one of the major disadvantages of this top-down approach to modeling regional development is in analyzing policy shocks. In this regard, it is important to assess whether the impact of a regional policy should have some effect on the national economy, since it is clear that the location of people and economic activity has an impact on the national economy" (p. 175). It is also possible, as in the case of Polenske's MRIO model, to exaggerate the virtue of internal consistency. A national projection could turn out to be entirely correct, but all the regional projections could turn out to be wrong by wide margins with positive and negative errors summing to zero.

The model is a large one, having 571 endogenous and 149 exogenous variables. An energy demand submodel contains 255 endogenous and 248 exogenous variables, while a population model includes approximately 800 variables. In spite of these impressive numbers, the model is not highly disaggregated, either industrially or spatially. There are only six blocks of industry equations, and the regions chosen are the nine Census regions.

The MGA model was tested by means of conventional "backcasts" covering the period 1963–1974 and calculations of mean absolute percentage errors. Given the high level of spatial and industrial aggregation, some of the errors seem rather large. GRP errors for the East South Central and Pacific regions, for example, were 3.26 and 3.83. The model did somewhat better in estimating total employment for most regions, although the Pacific error was 3.43. Personal income errors were 4.45 for the Pacific region and 5.02 for New England. Manufacturing wage rate errors were better with a high of 2.08 in the Pacific region. The performance of the energy model also was not outstanding. Residential energy consumption errors were greater than 3 percent in three regions, while the same errors in the industrial sector were larger than 3 percent in four regions, with a high of 5.15 in New England [159, p. 180].

It might strike some readers as carping criticism to regard errors of 3 percent as "high." But if a model dealing with broad industrial and geographic aggregates cannot get closer than 3 percent with actual data, it will certainly generate much larger errors when used to make forecasts.

The relative simplicity, and high levels of aggregation, of the MGA model makes it an ideal instrument for policy simulation. It was used to make projections to 1989 assuming major reductions in corporate and personal income taxes, decontrol of oil and gas prices, and a "less restrictive" monetary policy. Three national growth rates were projected. The model generated below-average increases in GRP and total employment for the "Northern Tier" states (not specifically defined), with above-average increases in the rest of the nation. If the "Northern Tier" includes the New England, Middle Atlantic, and East and West North Central regions, there is surprisingly little variation among regions in this two-way split of the national economy [p. 159, 183].

The energy-simulating exercise reaches the interesting conclusion that differentials in relative energy prices will narrow after 1984 because, among other things, "as wellhead prices increase, the transportation differential between regions becomes less important because it constitutes a smaller proportion of the total delivered cost of the energy product" [159, p. 186]. This conclusion relies on the implicit— albeit very doubtful— assumption that domestic oil and gas will be the major source of energy after 1984.[12]

The MGA simulations follow conventional neoclassical reasoning. The authors assume, for example, a relative decline in wage rates in the "Northern Tier" and a relative rise elsewhere. This together with the assumption of a relative narrowing in energy prices among regions will "tend to encourage the convergence of growth rates" (p. 188).

These conclusions follow, of course, from the assumptions built into the model. The latter could be varied, however, and it would be interesting to see a set of simulations based on assumptions that differ significantly from those used.

THE PRESENT STATE OF THE ART

The last chapter concluded with the statement that, despite a widespread belief to the contrary, there is no truly "operational" multiregional input–output model. The point was made that this is not because of a deficiency in interregional or multiregional *models*. It is basically a data problem.

What can be said about the state of the art of regional and interregional econometric models? First, most econometric models are less demanding than input–output models in terms of data requirements. Input–output models are deterministic; that is, the equations describing interindustry relations do not include explicit error terms.[13]

It is probably too early to pass judgment on econometric models. The only *true* test of any model is its ability to perform satisfactorily. "Backcasts" tell us that a model has been well specified. But unless the underlying relationships of any economic system—regional, national, or international—remain unchanged, there is no *a priori* reason to expect econometric models to forecast as well as they backcast, and one of the more reliable truisms we can count on is that history does not repeat itself.

Econometric models are more flexible than input–output models. There is more room for systematic trial and error. Variables and equations can be added, tested, and either retained or dropped.[14]

Economic forecasting is always a hazardous art, even if one has available a model consisting of several hundred equations. But econometric models are not used only to make forecasts. Given the present state of the art, and the constant need for more and better regional data, it might be safer to use contemporary econometric models for simulation exercises, and various kinds of policy analysis. Glickman's Philadelphia model, for example, has been used for both purposes and has performed reasonably well. In many ways, the multiregional econometric models developed thus far strike one as being more primitive than the best of the strictly regional models.

Perhaps the most important point to be made about regional and interregional econometric models is that while they have come a long way, they still have a long way to go. This is anything but a counsel of despair. It is simply a realistic statement that much work remains to be done both to improve the theory of econometric model building and the quality of data use. The "ideal" econometric model will never be built. One can only hope that there will be continued progress and steady improvement.

NOTES

1. There are cases in which, for mathematical reasons, structural equations cannot be solved to obtain reduced forms. An illustration of such a case is given later in this chapter.
2. For further discussion, see Isserman [102] and Pleeter [172].
3. The Northeast Corridor includes New Hampshire, Massachusetts, Rhode Island, Connecticut, New York, New Jersey, Pennsylvania, Delaware, Maryland, the District of Columbia, and Virginia.
4. The subregions of the Northeast Corridor were defined as *the South,* (Delaware, Maryland, D.C., and Virginia); *the Center* (New York, New Jersey, and Pennsylvania); and the *Northern Sub-region* (remaining states).
5. The only part of Delaware in this valley is the Wilmington SMSA. All other counties (and SMSAs) are in Pennsylvania and New Jersey (cf. Ballard and Glickman [8, p. 162]).
6. Hall and Licari adapted the basic Glickman model to the Los Angeles SMSA using time-series extending from 1959 to 1970. They used this model to project output and employment by sector to 1976. They also calculated impact multipliers for selected exogenous and endogenous sectors, as well as aggregate income and employment multipliers [83, pp. 347–350].
7. The model described by Treyz will not be discussed here. While fully specified, it had not been estimated for this symposium. For a discussion of the model, and earlier work by Treyz and various associates, see Treyz's article [207, pp. 191–206].
8. See Ballard, Gustely, and Wendling [9] for a more detailed description of NRIES.
9. Bolton has referred to NRIES as a "hybrid" model, although in his relatively brief discussion [19, pp. 275–277] he does not indicate why he prefers this designation to that of a completely bottom-up model as described by Ballard and Wendling.
10. In the summary version of NRIES, mean absolute percent errors (MAPEs) were calculated for only five variables: resident employment, GSP in constant dollars, resident personal income in current dollars, resident population, and retail sales. The range of errors was small for the first four, in most cases being less than 2 percent. Retail sales errors were larger, with almost half greater than 3 percent. The largest was 5.59 percent. Ballard and Wendling conducted the tests by running a "dynamic simulation" for 1963–1973, then comparing actual with calculated state estimates. The authors point out that the variables tested are aggregates that benefit from compensating error when compared with individual sector variables [10, p. 151].
11. There are presently four versions of MRMI covering different geographic areas: (1) counties, (2) 173 Business Economic Areas (BEAs), (3) SMSAs and ROEAs (Rest-of-Economic Areas), and (4) DOT transportation zones.
12. The authors could have made the same assumption about coal shipments, however.

13. This is not to say that input–output models are error-free, but only that one cannot make explicit statements about the significance or nonsignificance of the parameters in input–output systems. The parameters of econometric models are calculated to include measures of significance as well as margins of statistical error in empirical versions of econometric equations.

14. This is not to suggest, or even imply, that the issue is one of econometric *versus* input–output models. Indeed, the "ideal" empirical model would be an input–output model conjoined with an econometric model. On this, see L'Esperance [121].

PART II

Regional Development: Problems and Policies

Chapter 3

Regional Development Policy in the United States

STATE AND LIMITED FEDERAL PROGRAMS

The first federal regional development program in the United States—the Tennessee Valley Authority (TVA)—was launched during the depressed 1930s. It was a specialized program, designed initially to exploit the potential of hydroelectric power [6, p. 36]. Although it was a long-range effort, conditions in the Tennessee Valley began to improve as soon as some of the multipurpose dams were completed. Not only did they bring low-cost electricity to the valley, they also controlled the floods, which had been a constant threat in the past.

The TVA was thought by its proponents to be a model for similar river valley development programs elsewhere, but even during the era of the New Deal there was enough concern among conservative groups about the expansion of public power projects to prevent replication of this experiment in other regions. There was to be a long hiatus before the federal government became involved in regional development activities again.

During World War II, economic problems were subordinated to the major objective of winning the war. And the momentum of the wartime economy, supported by a high level of personal savings and pent-up demand, lasted until 1948. That year marked the first of a number of relatively brief but severe recessions that hit the U.S. economy during the next dozen years. It became apparent that the regional impacts of these recessions were highly uneven. Some regions were hit much harder than others. After 1948, pockets of chronic, localized unemployment persisted in many areas, even during periods of national recovery from these recessions.

There were several causes of this localized unemployment. One was technological change, such as a substitution of diesel for steam locomotives engendered by low-cost imported oil. This change affected such centers as Altoona, Pennsylvania, which at one time was the largest steam-locomotive repair center in the United States. The shift from oil to coal also exacerbated the displacement of coal miners by mechanization, which resulted in widespread, persistent unemployment throughout the Appalachian and Midwest coal-producing regions.

A major cause of the emergence of depressed industrial areas, particularly in New England and the Middle Atlantic states, was the large-scale migration of the textile and hosiery industries to the South. While other factors no doubt contributed to this shift, the major cause was the attraction of low labor costs. Old mills in the North were allowed to run out, and they were typically closed during recessions, adding to the severity of those short-term declines. Meanwhile, new mills embodying the latest technical developments were being opened in the South.

The massive relocation of labor-oriented industries was primarily the result of interregional differences in factor prices. But it was also influenced by shifts in demand. New synthetic fabrics appeared on the market shortly after World War II, and most of the mills producing them were located in the South. Other factors contributed to the persistence of depressed areas, both in the industrial-urban Northeast, and in rural areas such as Appalachia. These included the depletion of resources, protracted seasonal unemployment, and rising imports.

The localized unemployment of the 1950s was not a new phenomenon. It was far more widespread after World War II, however, than it had been during earlier periods, when the national economy was growing extensively due to the availability of free land and the growth of new towns in the West. During the Great Depression chronic unemployment was ubiquitous, so the regional aspects of this problem received little attention. The distinguishing feature of the unemployment of the 1950s was that it persisted in good times and bad. Although the recessions that began in 1948 and continued throughout the following decade followed earlier cyclical patterns, the national unemployment rate was a bit higher after each recovery as the problem of localized unemployment spread.

The first efforts to cope with the problem of persistent, localized unemployment were at the state and local levels. Pennsylvania, for example, established an Industrial Development Authority in 1956. This agency was authorized to make loans covering as much as 30 percent of the cost of new industrial projects in the state. New Hampshire, Maine, and Rhode Island made similar efforts. By the late 1950s a survey conducted by the Committee for Economic Development revealed that there were more than 300 local redevelopment agencies and about 135 area development associations in the United States [131, p. 159].

During the early 1950s the federal government made limited efforts to provide aid to areas of substantial labor surplus. In 1952, for example, the Office of Defense Mobilization announced Defense Manpower Policy No. 4. Its objective was to channel government contracts to surplus labor areas. Most government procurement was conducted by the normal method of advertising for bids, with contracts awarded to the lowest qualified bidder. Defense Manpower Policy No. 4 provided for "set-asides" for certain products, particularly textiles, and those government orders were filled by negotiating bids with employers in labor-surplus areas. Predictably, manufacturers in low-cost areas objected to this policy, particularly when contracts were awarded to firms that could not match the lowest public bid. After November 1953, the policy was revised to require bidders to meet the lowest public bid. A second effort to aid establishments in labor-surplus areas was to grant certificates permitting accelerated amortization to qualified firms engaged in defense work.

The limited federal programs no doubt assisted specific communities. But as late as 1962, after Defense Manpower Policy No. 4 (as amended) had been in effect for a decade, only about 0.5 percent of total military procurement consisted of set-asides to establishments in labor-surplus areas. And by the same year, only 74 accelerated amortization certificates had been granted. The firms granted the rapid amortization privilege employed more than 17,000 workers [131, p. 161], but there is no way of estimating the proportion of jobs that were created by this program.

The initial reaction to the spreading problem of localized unemployment was that it was a local, or at most, a state, responsibility. The first public organization to take the position that depressed industrial areas constituted a *national* problem—and thus required national action—was the National Planning Association. It issued a policy statement to that effect in January 1957 [139]. Conservative business organizations, such as the U.S. Chamber of Commerce, took issue with this statement. They insisted that local problems were a matter for local political jurisdictions to handle.

By the mid-1950s it had become apparent that piecemeal efforts limited to establishments engaged in defense work were having relatively little effect on chronic, localized unemployment. In 1955, the Senate Committee on Labor and Public Welfare appointed a subcommittee to investigate the causes of high-level localized unemployment. Later that year, the Senate Committee on the Economic Report authorized the study of low-income families. As a result of these investigations, and of the National Planning Association's study, Senator Paul H. Douglas of Illinois introduced a bill that would have established an independent Depressed Area Administration with the authority to make loans to firms willing to locate or expand in labor-surplus areas. The initial Douglas Bill made little headway, but during the second session of the 84th Congress, Douglas introduced another bill that would have provided aid to both industrial and rural redevelopment areas. It passed the Senate by a two-to-one majority, but it failed to pass the House of Representatives.

Between 1956 and 1961, depressed-area legislation was introduced in every session of Congress. Two of these bills passed both the Senate and the House only to be vetoed by President Eisenhower. Supporters of depressed-area legislation were unable to muster enough votes to override the vetoes (see Levitan, [124]). But the issue of federal aid to depressed areas became important in the presidential campaign of 1960. John F. Kennedy promised that if elected he would urge Congress to provide federal aid to labor-surplus areas, and the first piece of major legislation he signed after becoming President—on May 1, 1961—was the Area Redevelopment Act (ARA).

EARLY NATIONAL POLICY: THE AREA REDEVELOPMENT ACT

The Area Redevelopment Act differed greatly from the limited programs, whether federal, local, or state, described earlier. The limited programs were judged by their local effects. Under them, gains in employment in some areas could easily be at the expense of other areas. The Area Redevelopment Administration, however, was not intended to be a clearinghouse for shifting jobs. Indeed, the terms of the act specifically precluded this: "Under the provisions of this Act new employment opportunities should be created by developing and expanding new and existing facilities and resources rather than merely transferring jobs from one area of the United States to another" [131, p. 165].

The Area Redevelopment Act was the first legislation of its kind to recognize that persistent, localized unemployment, and persistent low incomes, are national rather than local or regional problems. The objective of the agency was to create *new* jobs. If new jobs could be added in depressed areas, without reducing employment elsewhere, both the communities involved and the nation would gain. This bottom-up approach, which is consistent with the objective of maximizing national product, is the only justification for regional development programs in the eyes of neoclassical economists (see, e.g., Borts [20, p. 184]).

The new act established the Area Redevelopment Administration in the U.S. Department of Commerce. Under the law, a "redevelopment area" could be designated by the Secretary of Commerce if unemployment in the area had been: (a) 50 percent above the national average for three of four preceding years, (b) 75 percent above the national average for two of the three preceding years, or (c) twice the national average for one of the two preceding years. Areas that did not meet these requirements, but in which there was an unusually high proportion of low-income families, could also be designated. Within two years more than a thousand areas had been designated as eligible for ARA assistance. They included about one-fifth of the nation's population, and accounted for approximately 27 percent of national unemployment [131, p. 165].

Since the Area Redevelopment Administration represented a new direction in U.S. public policy, it had no domestic precedent to draw on. The director and his staff were familiar with British efforts to deal with similar problems, however, and the British experience shaped both the new law and its administration.[1] Essentially, the ARA was involved in a program of *directly productive investment* (DPI). The principal forms of aid provided by the law were loans to business establishments, and loans or grants to communities to assist them in developing new enterprises.

The ARA was a modest regional development program, given the scope of the depressed-area problem. During its first three years of operation, it authorized 478 redevelopment projects that, the agency estimated, employed 28,100 persons. It had spent a total of $254 million during that period. About 54 percent of the total represented industrial and commercial loans, and 35 percent had gone to communities in the form of public facility loans or grants. The remaining 11 percent represented expenditures for technical assistance, and an embryonic training program later shifted to the Department of Labor.[2]

Critics of the Area Redevelopment Act gave the program relatively low marks (see, e.g., Levitan [124] and Newman [166]). The critics might have expected more than the ARA, given its limited resources and the large number of eligible areas, could possibly have delivered.

A 1963 survey of 33 establishments representing a cross-section of ARA-funded projects supported the ARA administrator's claims that the program was working.

The survey compared characteristics of the workers employed in plants supported by ARA loans with those of the workers in a sample of plants at "market-induced" locations. The survey showed that 43 percent of the workers in the ARA sample had been unemployed at the time they found their new jobs, compared with 16 percent in the "market-induced" sample. Only 35 perent of the workers in the ARA sample were employed at the time they moved to their new jobs, compared with 67 percent in the "market-induced" sample. The survey also showed that about 44 percent of the workers in the ARA sample had upgraded their skills and were earning more on their current jobs than they had in the past.[3]

Studies conducted after the ARA was no longer in operation also showed that some of the multiplier effects anticipated by the ARA's supporters did indeed take place. In one instance at least, an industrial development program started in Arkansas had the effect of shifting one community from a labor-surplus to a labor-shortage area, attracting new entrants and in-migrants to the ARA-supported establishment, and to other establishments attracted to the area by the first plant located there [148, p. 180, and the references cited].

Perhaps the strongest evidence that the ARA was working, however, was the hostility that the agency engendered, particularly in the House of Representatives. While scholars criticized the ARA for its limited successes, representatives of businesses in areas where ARA-supported establishments were operating successfully were complaining bitterly to their congressmen about the "unfair competition" of government-subsidized establishments. Indeed, it is at least possible, if not probable, that the major cause of the ARA's demise was that it worked too well rather than too poorly.

A SHIFT IN EMPHASIS: THE ECONOMIC DEVELOPMENT ADMINISTRATION

The Area Redevelopment Act was superseded in 1965 by the Public Works and Economic Development Act (EDA).[4] The EDA differed from the ARA in a number of important respects. Both acts were designed to assist areas and regions of substantial and consistent unemployment and underemployment, but while the ARA limited its assistance to small and medium-sized communities, the EDA became involved in problems of urban areas as well as those of smaller communities.

One of the communities designated for assistance by the EDA— possibly as a trial balloon—was Oakland, California. The Oakland experiment was far from a success. It generated a considerable amount of controversy, particularly after two scholars from the University of California—Jeffrey L. Pressman and Aaron D. Wildavsky—published a book, *Implementation*, highly critical of the experiment [181].

While theirs is a serious book, Pressman and Wildavsky appended a long subtitle clearly designed as an eye-catcher: "How Great Expectations in Washington Are Dashed in Oakland; or, Why It's Amazing That Federal Programs Work at All. This Being a Saga of the Economic Development Administration as Told by Two Sympathetic Observers Who Seek to Build Morals on a Foundation of Ruined Hopes." Needless to say, this whimsical subtitle was not appreciated by officials, either in Oakland or Washington. Available evidence supports the Pressman–Wildavsky conclusion [141, pp. 390–394]. Whatever else it might have accomplished, the EDA quite clearly was not the answer to the nation's urban problems. Nor was it intended to be by its original sponsors.

The Economic Development Administration, like its predecessor, was responsible for the administration of two basic programs. The local public works program, which accounted for about two-thirds of the EDA's total expenditures by early 1978, was not related to the regional development program. But the latter also consisted of two major parts: public works and business development loans.

During the first seven years of its operation, 66 percent of the EDA's expenditures went for public works while only 13 percent were in the form of business loans. The most notable difference between the ARA and the EDA was the shift from investment in directly productive activities (DPI) to investment in social overhead capital (SOC). This was no doubt a response to the "unfair competition" criticism of the ARA.

It is more difficult to estimate the impacts of investment in social overhead capital than directly productive investment. In an effort to measure the effectiveness of the EDA, expenditures per capita by state were related to changes in per capita income and changes in the unemployment rate [142, p. 4]. The overall relationship was not particularly close: the rank correlation coefficient between EDA expenditures and changes in per capita income was only .31, and that between expenditures and changes in the unemployment rate was only .17 [142, p. 3]. At the state level it appeared that the EDA had had little effect on either per capita income or unemployment. More will be said about the problems and performance of the EDA after a discussion of the third regional development program, which was a product of the Kennedy–Johnson era.

APPALACHIA: AN EXPERIMENT IN FEDERAL–STATE COOPERATION

Parts of the region now known as Appalachia have deep historical roots, having been among the first areas settled during the post-Colonial era. But the original boundaries of the Appalachian region were drawn in 1965 when the Appalachian Regional Development Act (ARDA) was passed. The boundaries were later expanded as additional states were included in the program.[5] One state, West Virginia, and parts of twelve others, are included in modern-day Appalachia.

This region is far from homogeneous. There are three rather clearly defined subregions, Northern, Central, and Southern (see Figure 3–1). But even the subregions are not entirely homogeneous in terms of social and economic characteristics. There are, however, certain physical and economic features which determined the boundaries of Appalachia. For instance, it includes the most mountainous parts of the United States east of the Mississippi River. It accounts for 23 percent of the land area, and 21 percent of the population, of this part of the nation. There are still many small farms in the region, but it produces only 14 percent of the value of the farm output east of the Mississippi [5, p. 74]. It is a region rich in resources: all the nation's anthracite coal, and most of its high-grade metallurgical coal, is located here. It also has enormous reserves of steam coal, and is well endowed with limestone. It was thus a natural location for many of the nation's original steel mills.

Most of the counties in Appalachia had the following economic characteristics in common in 1965: low per capita income, high and persistent unemployment, declining population, relatively low levels of educational attainment, and above-average incidences of malnutrition and other conditions that accompany poverty. At the same time, the region included the nation's leading steel-producing center (Pittsburgh), and one of its major chemical-producing areas (in the Kanawha Valley of West Virginia).

The causes of economic distress in Appalachia are detailed in New man's excellent book, *The Political Economy of Appalachia* [166]. One series of events must be mentioned explicitly since the effects were sudden and devastating. Following the end of World War II, the railroads, the utility companies, and many manufacturing establishments suddenly switched from coal to fuel oil. John L. Lewis, leader of the United Mine Workers, realized that the coal industry could survive only through a major shift in production practices. He took the lead in negotiating an agreement, in 1950, which not only permitted but

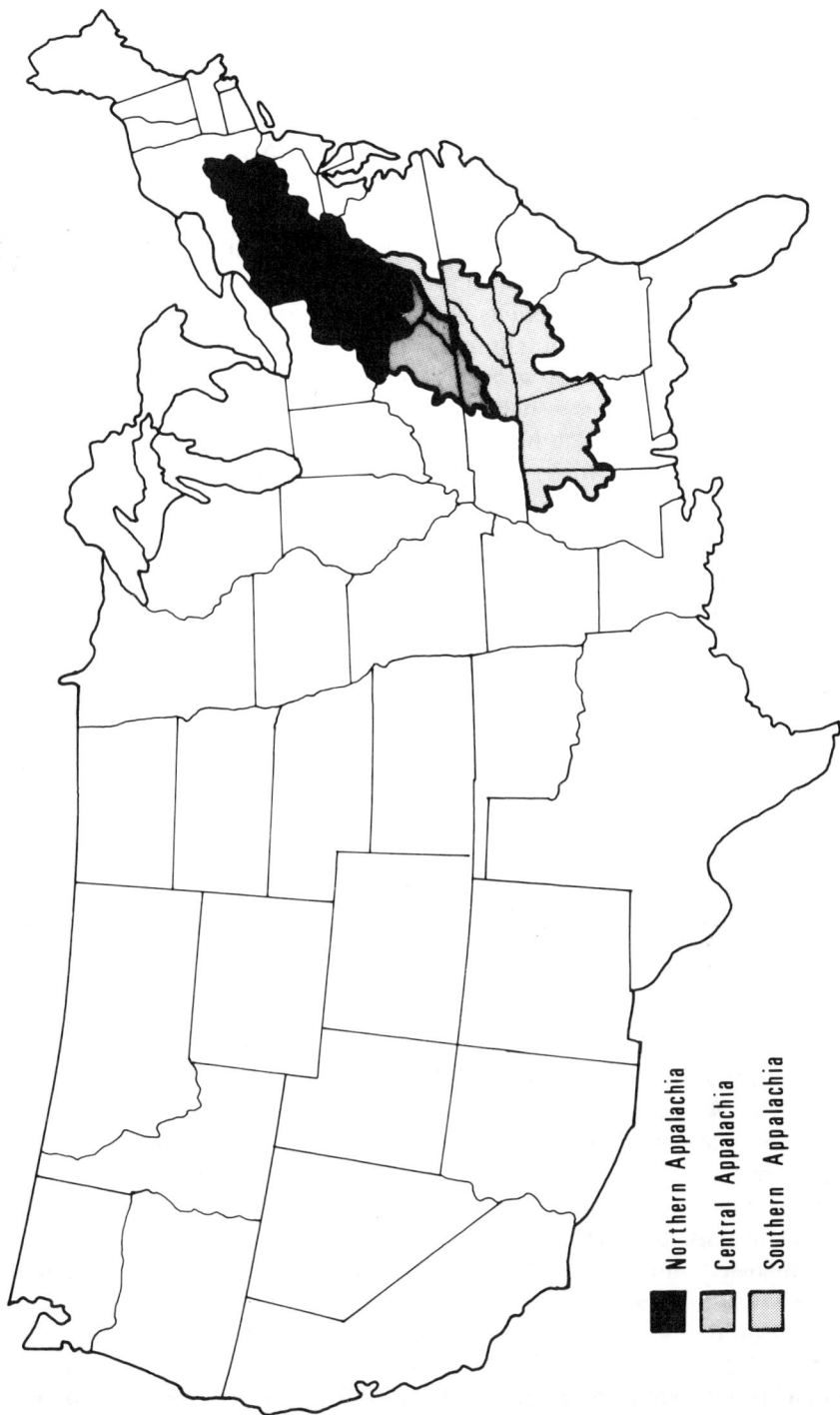

Northern Appalachia

Central Appalachia

Southern Appalachia

Source: 1977 Annual Report, Appalachian Regional Commission.

Figure 3–1. Appalachia.

encouraged mechanization of the mines. As a consequence, while coal production in the nation declined 25 percent, from 535 tons in 1951 to 403 tons in 1961, employment declined from 400,000 to 144,000, or 64 percent. The social and economic consequences on the region of this massive dislocation of workers were devastating [136].

During the 1960 presidential campaign, Appalachia was "rediscovered" as the nation's most seriously depressed area. About two years later, a group of governors representing Appalachian states formed the Conference of Appalachian Governors. Their objective was a joint federal–state program to revive the stagnant Appalachian economy. President Kennedy responded by establishing the President's Appalachian Regional Commission (PARC), which devoted a year to a study of the region's economic problems.

The committee report recommended three major economic goals: (1) improved access to the rest of the economy; (2) increased use of the region's natural resources, including its water resources; and (3) investment in educational and health facilities. On March 9, 1965, President Johnson signed the bill establishing the Appalachian Regional Commission (ARC). The new law followed rather closely the recommendations of PARC.

The Appalachian Regional Commission represented a new departure in the American political system. It was the first *joint* federal–state agency. It was administered by a federal cochairman, appointed by the President, and a state cochairman, a position that rotated among the participating governors. An office was established in Washington, D.C. with a relatively small staff.

The original federal appropriation was not large—$1,069 million. More than 77 percent of this amount was earmarked for a Development Highway System, with east–west highways designed to interstate standards, to supplement the predominantly north–south interstate highways. The law was somewhat flexible about state matching funds. Some states were required to contribute 50 percent of the cost of highways while others contributed only 30 percent. The same range applied to other programs. Thus combined federal and state appropriations ranged somewhere between $1.5 and $1.9 billion. After customary bureaucratic delays, the Appalachian Regional Development program was in full swing by the late 1960s.

The heavy emphasis on highway construction was criticized by some economists, who proposed instead major investments in human capital—in health and educational facilities—that would, they argued, give the residents of this depressed region a better opportunity to compete for jobs in other parts of the country. This advice was disregarded, however, and the ARC continued to devote most of its resources to the Development Highway System until the completion of the system was assured. It was at that point—by the mid-1970s—that the ARC shifted its emphasis to investment in health and educational facilities.

Through repeated extensions of the original act, the Appalachian Regional Development program was kept alive, although the Reagan administration indicated, early in 1981, that it had plans to dismantle the ARC.[6] By February 1979, 73 percent of the projected 2,384 miles of development highways had been completed or were under construction, and 86 percent of the planned access roads had been finished or were being built. During that time, 1,272 demonstration health programs had been initiated, at a cost of almost $422 million. More than a thousand vocational educational facilities had been established, at a cost of $332 million. Smaller sums were expended for other health facilities, higher education facilities, and libraries, and about $195 million was spent on some 800 water pollution control programs [6].

SUMMING UP

What can be said, in summary, about the three redevelopment programs discussed in this chapter? The Area Redevelopment Administration program has been evaluated, if that term can be applied to the impressionistic statements made in an earlier section. But how do the Economic Development program and the ARC program compare? In terms of stated objectives, the ARC would have to be rated as a more successful program than the EDA (see Miernyk [141, 142]). Both the ARC and the EDA relied primarily on social overhead capital investments to achieve their stated goals. But the Appalachian region benefited from exogenous forces—the rapid rise of energy prices during the 1970s—which resulted in the revival of some of the more severely depressed parts of the region. While there is no doubt that the development highways, and the various forms of investment in human capital, have contributed to the revival of Appalachia, the gains in this region would have been much smaller in the absence of the "energy crisis." More will be said about the success of the Appalachian program in the next several pages.

The EDA's investment in local public facilities and amenities— which account for the vast bulk of its total expenditures—are much harder to evaluate. Communities that received local public facility grants are undoubtedly better places in which to live, and possibly even in which to do business, than they would have been otherwise. But there is little evidence that such investment has had significant impacts on regional economic development. There is no way any of the regional development programs can be labeled as clear-cut "failures," although one of the extensions of EDA, to be discussed in Chapter 4, is hard to defend. The EDA was also marked for extinction by the Reagan administration, which proposed to ease the political pain that such a move might engender by substituting block grants to the states. Past experience shows that block grants are rarely used for development purposes. As in the case of the ARC, shutting down the EDA would require congressional approval.

INTERNAL AND EXTERNAL INFLUENCES
IN APPALACHIAN RECOVERY

There have been substantial changes in Appalachia since 1965. In that year, per capita personal income averaged $2,178, or 78.2 percent of the U.S. average. By 1976, Appalachian per capita income had more than doubled, and stood at 84.8 percent of the U.S. average [5, p. 56]. There was still substantial variation within the region. In northern Appalachia, for example, per capita income had increased from 86.6 percent of the U.S. average to 90.4 percent; in southern Appalachia the increase had been from 73 percent to 80.8 percent. Central Appalachia—the hard core of the region's depressed counties in 1965—registered an increase from 52 percent to 72 percent of the U.S. average during this period [5, p. 56].

Other indexes show relative improvement in Appalachia's position. Before 1971, for example, the unemployment rate in the entire region remained well above the national average. Between 1971 and 1977, however, unemployment rates in southern and central Appalachia were below the U.S. average [5, p. 43].

In 1960, more than 31 percent of Appalachian households were considered to be below the "poverty level," as defined by the Social Security Administration. This compared with the U.S. average of 22.1 percent. By 1970, the Appalachian proportion had dropped to 18.1 percent, while the U.S. average was down to 13.7 percent: the spread had narrowed by 4.7 percentage points [5, p. 66]. Finally, out-migration was reversed after 1970. The population of Appalachia increased 5.4 percent between 1970 and 1976 while the U.S. population went up 5.2 percent. The gain in Appalachia included net in-migration of about 380,000 people [6].

The available data show that the economy of Appalachia has improved vis-à-vis the U.S. economy since 1965. The interesting question is, how much of this improvement is due to the Appalachian Regional Development program and how much is the result of exogenous influences? There is no definitive answer. Both the program and external influences have contributed to the economic resurgence of the region. While one cannot assign weights to the various forces contributing to the improvement of the Appalachian economy, it is easy to identify the most important external changes that affected it.

Two global events had a major impact on the development of Appalachia. First, the region's "favorable" showing is actually due, in part, to the unfavorable growth record of the U.S. economy since the early 1970s. The second influence is the revolutionary change in the structure of energy prices, which started in the late 1960s and accelerated sharply after 1974. Since most of the coal produced in the eastern United States comes from Appalachia, this region benefited from the sharp increase in coal prices, which began in 1971.

Until 1971, the average price of Appalachian coal had held steady, at well under $5 per ton, for many years. By 1978, the average price was in the neighborhood of $29 per ton, a fivefold increase.[7] (The average price in West Virginia was $33.15 per ton that year, but since West Virginia produces more metallurgical coal than the other Appalachian states, the average price of its coal is higher than the regional average.) Appalachia has clearly gained from this shift, and is likely to gain more in the future if energy prices continue to rise more rapidly than the general price level.

One possible outcome of the shifting terms of trade between energy producers and energy consumers is the strengthening of the industrial base of energy-producing states. This will come at the expense of other industrialized states, which must import their energy in one form or another. Appalachia ia already more heavily industrialized than the nation as a whole. As early as 1970, for example, 33.7 percent of total employment in the region was in manufacturing, compared to a U.S. average of 25.9 percent. Indeed, Appalachia has an above-average share of all major manufacturing industry-groups except four: machinery, except electrical; food and beverages; motor vehicles and transportation equipment; and printing and publishing [5, p. 51]. The industries that are not heavily represented in Appalachia are not particularly energy-intensive; some of the other industry groups already well represented in the region, however, do involve energy-intensive activities. Industries such as steel, chemicals, and aluminum—already an important part of the region's industrial base—could expand.

Coal production in Appalachia has been expanding slowly in recent years, and the outlook is for further growth. There will be only one direction in which the United States can turn for additional basic energy in the near term, and that is to its most abundant source, coal.

This augurs well for the economic future of Appalachia. The regional tendencies described above—the relative shift of income from energy-importing to energy-producing regions—is almost certain to continue.

A complex set of factors have contributed to the revival of Appalachia. It is difficult to assess the impact of the Appalachian Regional Development program on the region. My judgment is that exogeneous influences have had more to do with the economic revival than the program. But the development highway system, the improvements in educational facilities, and the expansion and improvement of health care services have made important contributions. The various causes complement each other; they do not in any way conflict.

Finally, the Appalachian region has a long way to go to achieve parity with the United States in terms of average income per person, and there are still serious problems of distribution. The urban areas of Appalachia—including small cities and large towns—show the effects of improvement in income and decline in unemployment. But in some of the rural areas, and on the outskirts of many cities and towns, there is still evidence of serious economic deprivation. The scars of almost two decades of severe depression, at a time when the national economy was enjoying buoyant growth, will not be eradicated quickly. It will be easier to deal with the remaining pockets of poverty in the future, however, if the general economic health of the region continues to improve.

NOTES

1. For a discussion of the British experience, see Miernyk [133, 134, 143].
2. This brief review of the ARA's activities is limited to the regional development aspects of the act. Under the Accelerated Public Works Act of 1962, the ARA was given the operational reponsibility for administering a contra-cyclical program, which was much broader than the regional development program. By the end of 1963, the agency had administered 4,646 public works projects with an estimated completion value of $285 million. Thus, the "side activity" of the agency was larger than its basic regional development program.
3. For further details on this survey and its findings, see Miernyk [148], especially pp. 168–182.
4. Public Law 89-136, 89th Congress, 1st Session (August 26, 1965).
5. See Appalachian Regional Commission [6], pp. 2–7, and Newman [166], pp. 26–31.
6. That could be done, of course, only with congressional concurrence. The latest extension of the act was scheduled to expire in September 1982.
7. The effects of the shifting "terms of trade" between energy-producing and energy-consuming states have been analyzed elsewhere [140].

Chapter 4

Resource Constraints and Regional Development Policy

INTRODUCTION

Regional development policies in the United States—as well as those in Great Britain, several Western European countries, and some countries in South America—were formulated at a time when economists and policy makers focused almost exclusively on demand considerations. The task, as it was then envisaged, was to stimulate the regional demand for resources—especially human resources—that were in excess supply. Out of this approach came a variety of programs to encourage investment in depressed areas. In most countries, regional development policies presupposed continued growth of the national economy. Specific policies were designed in some countries to direct part of the new investment ensured by growth to areas of above-average employment and below-average income.

In the United States, the initial approach, discussed in Chapter 3, was one of direct public investment in productive facilities in depressed areas, with the proviso that these facilities were not to be built at the expense of similar facilities in other regions. In Great Britain, by contrast, the policy was one of directing new investment away from crowded areas to those with excess labor. Similarly, Brazil developed a unique fiscal incentive program to shift investment from the expanding South to the lagging North. Later, in the United States, under the Economic Development Administration, policy shifted from direct investment to investment in public facilities in development areas. This, it was hoped, would stimulate the private sector to invest in those areas.[1] In all cases, however, the emphasis was on stimulating aggregate effective demand—in the Keynesian sense—in development areas.

This chapter will evaluate those policies within the framework of emerging supply constraints. Georgescu-Roegen's entropic bioeconomic analysis of the economic process, discussed more fully in Chapter 7, is used as a background for the evaluation of the regional policies that emerged in the 1960s. It concludes with a discussion and critique of changes made during the Carter administration, and with the direction—as I see it—that future regional policy should take.

REGIONAL GROWTH THEORIES

There are various ways to classify regional growth theories. One is to divide them into "competitive" and "generative" classes. Competitive theories view regional growth as a zero-sum game: there's only so much growth in the system, and it is "distributed" among regions according to the rules of conventional neoclassical theory. National economic growth is determined, and the distribution of real gross national product per capita—the variable customarily used to define economic growth—is decided by the competitive (or comparative) advantages or disadvantages of specific regions.

Generative growth theory, on the other hand, maintains that the national growth rate is the algebraic sum of changes in gross regional product per capita. This is a "bottom-up" approach. A certain amount of real output will be generated in each region, and gross national product is the sum of the regional totals. Changes in gross regional product in a generative regional model need not be positive. Some regions could grow, but others could experience absolute declines. If the declines outweigh the increases, gross national product would decline.

During the transition from the 1960s to the 1970s, growth rates in most industrialized nations of the world dropped, some quite sharply [162, p. 8]. The forces of inflation, clearly evident by the mid-1960s, accelerated as productivity declined. The widespread decline of economic growth, which is quite independent of political and economic systems, is often attributed to the "energy crisis" associated with the OPEC oil embargo of late 1973. But growth rates had dropped visibly in the United States, Japan, the Soviet Union, Great Britain, and other industrialized nations several years before the embargo.

The rising costs of oil and other fossil fuels have undoubtedly exacerbated the problem of slow economic growth. It would be a gross oversimplification, however, to attribute declining growth rates to any single cause. This widespread phenomenon is the result of a complex of causes, some of which are touched on later in this chapter. As noted in the preceding section, however, economic development policies in the United States were initiated during a decade of rapid and sustained economic growth. There is no evidence that policy makers at that time suspected that this condition might not last indefinitely.

THE CLARK–FISHER HYPOTHESIS UNDER EMERGING SUPPLY CONSTRAINTS

Regional disparities in per capita income, which were quite wide in 1929, have been narrowing steadily. The reasons for this are discussed in Chapter 7, and thus are only summarized here. Relative increases in per capita income in below-average regions have been typically associated with structural change, with long-run shifts from agriculture to industry, and subsequently to tertiary, or trade and service, activities. This association was postulated by Colin Clark, A. G. B. Fisher, and, at the regional level, Louis Bean [13, 36, 57]. The causes of Clark–Fisher structural change are capital accumulation, technological progress, and increases in productivity engendered by the latter [155, pp. 77–79].

The Clark–Fisher relationship, which seems to have been taken for granted in an earlier day, appears to be breaking down.[2] Regions now gaining in relative per capita income are abundantly endowed with fossil fuels and agricultural resources. The regions with declining relative per capita income are the older industrial regions and regions heavily dependent on tertiary activities.

The most rapid convergence occurred during the 1940s, reflecting the regional impacts of World War II and events of the immediate postwar period. The trend toward convergence slowed down after 1950. There was even divergence from the national average in some regions, notably New England and the Rocky Mountains. Since 1969, however, these two regions resumed their convergence toward the national average, moving in opposite directions (see Figure 7–3, p. 103).

Neoclassical regional economists feel that convergence supports their version of regional growth theory. It is, in their view, the result of regional differences in factor payments. Capital is attracted to regions with below-average wage rates and above-average returns to investors. Over time, they argue, the relocation of economic activity will produce convergence. Presumably, spatial equilibrium, in the sense of Pareto optimality, will be reached in the neoclassical model when per capita income is equal in all regions.

Is there any evidence that regional development programs in the United States have accelerated the rate of convergence? If there is, it's far from clear-cut. Per capita income in New England, which received a considerable amount of regional development assistance after 1960, continued to decline relative to the national average. And the trend in the Southwest, another area that has benefited from substantial regional development efforts, has been almost linear since 1950. The evidence is simply inconclusive.

Most economists are incurable optimists. They no doubt see what I regard as a new "trend" as nothing more than a short-term deviation from the "true" long-run trend. Once the energy riddle is solved, they assure us, we'll be back on the turnpike of robust growth. If this happens, the Clark–Fisher relationship will reassert itself. But an opposite view is supported by the seminal work of Nicholas Georgescu-Roegen, who has developed an explanation of the economic process based on the laws of physics and thermodynamics, not on transitory relationships or human institutions.[3]

Historically, analyses of the development process, whether national or regional, have focused on demand. This has been particularly true during the Keynesian and the present post-Keynesian eras. Georgescu's work stresses the importance of supply constraints. This, of course, was the essence of the Malthusian doctrine. But the Malthusian forecast of impending doom as the growth of population outstripped the food supply was rendered nugatory by technological progress. Technology became a critical variable in all conventional economic growth models. But conventional economics implicitly assumes unlimited supplies of energy; supply constraints are not taken into account in neoclassical or post-Keynesian growth models.

Georgescu-Roegen breaks with conventional economic theory by pointing out that economic activity is not a circular flow. The economic growth process is one of cumulative and irreversible change. Economic systems, as they expand, are constantly transforming the world's stock of available energy from its *free* form to *bound* energy, which eventually is dissipated as heat and cannot be used again [70, p. 7]. Georgescu has also argued that critically important materials can be analyzed in entropic terms. There are also material as well as energy supply constraints on economic growth [74].

Events of the past decade offer no support for the position of technological optimists, who believe that we can return to the rapid growth rates of the 1960s. Their "technological fixes" seem to lie beyond ever-receding horizons. The technological optimists haven't tried to answer Georgescu-Roegen's arguments—they simply ignore them. Those of us who find his arguments to be convincing feel that his analysis explains the declining growth rates of the world's industrialized nations. Moreover, it leads to the conclusion that further declines in growth rates are inevitable. Such declines, in turn, will have profound consequences for regional development policy.

THE EDA'S TITLE V COMMISSIONS

As noted in the preceding chapter, the three regional programs launched during the Kennedy and Johnson administrations differed in a number of ways. But all were designed to assist "lagging regions"—defined as those with below-average family income and above-average unemployment rates—to share in the bounty that the robust growth of the 1960s was creating for the nation.

The first of these programs, the Area Redevelopment Administration, was widely regarded as a failure.[4] But those early judgments might have been premature. It would be hard to support an argument that the ARA was a howling success, but it did make some lasting contributions to regional development.[5] Indeed, in some ways, the ARA might have been too successful. Its focus was on investment in directly productive activities, which some members of Congress felt were "unfairly" competitive with private enterprise. Thus when the Economic Development Administration (EDA) was established to replace the ARA, emphasis shifted from investment in plant and equipment (via loans and grants to private companies) to investment in social overhead capital [141].

The Appalachian Regional Commission was also concerned with investment in social overhead capital, especially during the early stages of its operation. Indeed, most of its early expenditures were devoted to the construction of a development highway system. The objective was to link the predominantly east–west development highways to the interstate highways, and thus to integrate this largely bypassed region with the rest of the national economy. Although the decision to focus on highway construction was criticized during the early days of the ARC, it now seems evident that it was right at the time.[6]

The expansion of the Regional Action Planning Commissions (authorized by Title V of the Economic Development Act of 1965) during the Carter administration represented the final stage of regional development policies started in the 1960s. These commissions provide, in my view, a case study of regional development policy run amok. Section 501 of the Economic Development Act authorized the Secretary of Commerce, with the concurrence of the states concerned, "to designate economic development regions." The regions involved had to be made up of contiguous states, and there had to be some "geographical, cultural, historical, and economical" relationship among them. But the essential condition was *"that the region has lagged behind the Nation as a whole in economic development on the basis of such factors as unemployment rates, family incomes, living conditions, the decline of dominant industries, the out-migration of labor, adversely changing technology or national defense expenditures, and relative growth rates"* [212, p. 17, emphasis added].

The meaning of Section 501 is unequivocal. There was, however, no great rush to implement this section of the act. In 1966–67, five Regional Action Planning Commissions were designated: the Coastal Plains, Four Corners, New England, Ozarks, and Upper Great Lakes. Each region met the criteria established by Section 501, at least marginally. Cochairmen were appointed for each commission: a federal representative, and rotating representatives from each of the states.

The model of the Title V Commissions was the Appalachian Regional Commission. There are some important differences, however. The ARC had a Washington headquarters and a staff that over the years had attracted qualified professionals in a number of fields. The Title V Commissions, and their staffs, operated only in their designated regions. What the commission staffs did was always something of a mystery.

By the early 1970s, parts of the Appalachian development highway system were completed, and some of the growth centers served by these highways and the newly completed interstates appeared to be thriving. There were still many depressed communities and rural areas in Appalachia, but by the mid-1970s it was clear that Appalachia was beginning to catch up with the rest of the country. The primary reason, of course, was the revival of the coal industry, which brought sharp increases in coal prices and revenues. These changes had favorable effects on per capita income in the region. But the highways and vocational education facilities had contributed to industrial development in some parts of the region. Also, perhaps as important as anything, the ARC had established a clear regional identity. The picture of a people trapped in drab, hopeless poverty gave way to one of a region on the rebound.

There is no similar record of *regional* accomplishment in the Title V regions. Among regional economists, regional scientists, and others with an interest in regional affairs, the idea had spread that the New England Commission was the "best" of the Title Vs. But in October 1972, the *Boston Globe* ran a series of articles about the New England Regional Commission, which characterized it as "a high-level pork barrel operation that has squandered millions of tax dollars on salaries, shelved studies, and barren programs" [24]. The *Globe* articles gave details about the high salaries of commission staff members and the sizable amounts paid to outside consultants. The tone of the four articles, which ran on consecutive days from October 8 through October 11, was entirely negative. One of the state alternates— members who are chosen to represent the governors when they are unable to attend commission meetings—stated to a *Globe* reporter, "The Commission is just a high level political boondoggle, a sophisticated pork barrel. . . ." There also was less than complete harmony, according to one of the articles, between some members of the commission and its executive director.

The articles, which to my knowledge were never challenged, make dreary reading for anyone committed to regionalism. But what is truly astonishing is that despite the complete lack of a record of positive accomplishment, and in view of the strong indictment contained in the *Globe* articles, there was a growing move in Washington to expand the number of commissions. The ultimate goal was a set of "wall-to-wall" commissions that would blanket the nation.

Two new Title V Commissions were established in 1972, the Old West, and the Pacific Northwest. In October 1976, the Secretary of Commerce designated the Southwest Border Economic Development Region. No more were established until the early months of 1979, when three additional regions were designated: the Mid-Atlantic, Mid-South, and Mid-America.

The revived interest in Title V Commissions was attributed to the White House Conference on Balanced Growth and Economic Development held in Washington from January 29 through February 2, 1978. There was "general agreement among the delegates that no massive new federal spending programs were needed" [222, p. 1]. But President Carter also indicated his intention to propose new legislation that would give "the opportunity for all states to participate in multi-state Regional Commissions . . ." [222, p. 12]. It is not at all clear why he reached this decision, for there is no evidence that the older Title V Commissions had served any useful purpose. Before turning to an evaluation of these commissions, I will briefly digress on the concept of *balanced growth* and its relation to regional development.

THE CONCEPT OF "BALANCED" REGIONAL GROWTH

The notion of balanced growth grew out of the early work of international development economists. Development economics is a new branch of economics, which came into existence rather abruptly after World War II. It was an outgrowth of efforts by the world's more prosperous nations to stimulate economic development in "backward" countries, now referred to more euphemistically as "less developed countries" or, more simply, as LDCs.

Development economists had to forge new analytical tools and concepts literally from scratch, although they were able to draw on the earlier work of economic historians, who, by the nature of their craft, had long been concerned with the problems of economic development. Two schools of thought emerged early in the new game of development economics; one advocated "unbalanced" growth, and the other supported the doctrine of "balanced" growth. This controversy spawned a burgeoning literature dealing with such recondite matters as the effects that "pecuniary" and "technological" externalities have on economic development. But the basic argument could be stripped to its essentials: should development resources be concentrated in one or a few sectors, or should they be spread more widely? Should investments be made in projects which "though unprofitable individually, would be profitable collectively"? [60, p. 241].[7]

Some protagonists of balanced growth wanted massive infusions of outside capital to modernize agriculture in the LDCs with simultaneous construction of an industrial base. They also advocated training facilities to staff the trade and service occupations, which they hoped would be created quickly.

Many economists—particularly regional economists—were skeptical about the notion of balanced growth. Harry Richardson, a leading regional growth theorist, wrote, for example, that "the doctrine of balanced regional growth both within and between regions does not make good economic sense, though it is easy enough to formulate abstract models that yield predictions of this kind" [187, p. viii]. Most economists concerned with development issues, either at the national or regional level, believed that the process of economic growth would proceed more surely and smoothly if it moved through a series of stages, although they also felt that future shifts from rural-agrarian to urban-industrial societies need not take as long as those of the past.

The concept of balanced growth briefly sketched above is the one that is embedded in the professional economic literature. It is not the one discussed here. A new concept of "balanced growth" emerged in the 1970s in a different policy context. It should not be confused with the older ideas, which were the products of a slower gestation as a body of economic development literature emerged. Those seeking analytical support for the doctrine of balanced *regional* growth will not find it in the development literature.

The new notion of balanced regional growth can best be phrased as a question: How can federal agencies, through their manifold connections with the private sector, stimulate economic growth in lagging regions without inhibiting economic growth in regions where it is now occurring? More briefly, and more specifically, how can federal policies stimulate growth without inflation in the Northeast (broadly defined) without inhibiting the robust growth recently experienced by the South and West?

Some regional economists are as skeptical of this concept of balanced growth as some development economists were of the older notion that sought to bring about rapid change in the structure of less developed economies. Before looking at reasons for this skepticism, however, let us discuss briefly another question, to help clear the air somewhat. Why the emphasis on federal policy in this definition of balanced growth? There are two reasons. First, that was the focus of discussion in some policy-making circles. For example, various coalitions of governors emerged, whose objective was to shift federal spending from the South and the West to the Northeast.[8] The second reason is that if the private sector could bring about "balanced" regional growth, it would already have started to do so. In fact, however, it was the private sector's response to sudden and dramatic changes in the structure of interregional costs—with corresponding impacts on regional comparative advantages—that had caused the problems that the advocates of the "new" balanced growth doctrine sought to redress.

A CRITIQUE OF AND SUGGESTED ALTERNATIVE TO TITLE V

A detailed evaluation of the seven Title V Commissions designated by 1972 was prepared by the Center for Social Analysis, State University of New York, Binghamton. Both principal authors, Benjamin Chinitz and Monroe Newman, are distinguished regional economists and regional scientists. Their undated report, *Title V Regional Commissions: An Evaluation*, was prepared for the Office of Regional Economic Coordination, U.S. Department of Commerce [35].

The report is more descriptive than analytical, and the authors leave the clear impression that they are sympathetic to the notion of "wall-to-wall" regional commissions. They state that the commissions they examined had been "useful political and public administrative agencies." But they also maintain that "they suffered from such resource anemia that they struggled to find something useful that related (sometimes vaguely) to their mandate" [35, p. 17].

Chinitz and Newman concede that "no commission has succeeded in accomplishing the legislative intent of bringing the overall allocation and administration of public funds—federal, state, and local—into conformity with a regional plan" [35, p. 17]. But they say that they are not surprised in view of the limited funding and authority of the commissions.

It is clear, of course, that not all regions can be "below average" in family income and "above average" in unemployment. These criteria—the key criteria in the designation of the original commissions—had to be abandoned as the Department of Commerce edged toward a policy of "wall-to-wall" commissions. It is interesting, however, that in the (undated) press releases announcing the designation of the three new regional commissions in early 1979, each press release indicated some of the respective region's economic "disadvantages." In one of the press releases, for example, the leading justification was that "there are intraregional disparities in unemployment." And the second justification listed is that "the region's industrial sector is undergoing long-term structural changes."

But there are intraregional disparities in unemployment in *every region*, no matter how that region in defined. And long-term structural change is characteristic of *any* dynamic economy. It is apparent that staff members assigned the responsibility for providing a rationale for the new commissions were straining mightily to meet the original criteria for designation of development regions. It is equally clear, however, that if the nation were to be blanketed with regional commission, the original criteria for designation would have to be discarded. If the reasons given for the designation of the newer regional commissions were interpreted from a strictly legalistic point of view, it is doubtful that they could qualify.

Chinitz and Newman do not try to build a case for the seven commissions on the basis of established records of accomplishment. Instead, they maintain, "The notion was (and still is in the minds of many) that the unique contribution of a Title V Commission would be the capacity to develop long-range regional plans which would identify the resources required from federal, state, and local sources to meet the region's development needs" [35, p. 5]. To Chinitz and Newman this is the heart of the matter. They go on to say that "no single federal agency and no single state government could do that job as well because of their limited perspectives and authorities."

It is clear that the authors of the Title V evaluation report had discarded the notion of regional commissions as vehicles of regional *development*. "There was further obfuscation," they write, "caused by the birth of the concept in the context of lagging regions. Why would a new approach to federalism be restricted to lagging regions? Therefore, it followed that the really important dimensions of Title V were the planning, the multiregional perspective, and the extra dollars justified in terms of regional lags" [35, p. 5]. The meaning of this statement escapes me, although I hasten to add that I am not accusing the authors of attempting even further obfuscation.

Chinitz and Newman wanted to recast the mission of the commissions. They saw them as useful administrative identities that would serve as intermediaries between the states and the federal government. I disagree. Instead of regional commissions, I favor a stronger regional office in the U.S. Department of Commerce. This office could work closely with the Federal Regional Councils (FRCs) established by Executive Order 11647 (February 10, 1972).[9] The FRCs could provide the interface between Washington and the states advocated by Newman and Chinitz as the proper role of the Title V Commissions. I appreciate the differences between the two sets of organizational structures, but the Standard Federal Regions (SFRs) and the FRCs can be taken as a *fait accompli*. Their existence supports the conclusion that the Title V Commissions had become totally superfluous.[10]

Long before it was a widely held view, I argued that regional distress was a *national* rather than local problem [139]. My views on this issue haven't changed, although years of study of regional development policies in the United States and a number of other countries have convinced me that the elimination of regional disparities in income and employment is one of the more intractable problems a democratic society faces. That doesn't mean society should stop trying.

The difficulties of assisting lagging regions under conditions of robust national economic growth are greatly compounded when the national growth rate turns down sharply, as it has in the United States and a number of other industrialized countries. The new era of slow growth will generate a host of new regional problems. And those problems will have to be viewed as national rather than local in character. The federal government will have to play a role—indeed the dominant role—in working toward the amelioration of regional problems. But it will do this most effectively by working through a strong regional office in Washington rather than through weak and ineffective agencies that are regional in name only.

NOTES

1. For a survey of the United States and European experience, see Hansen [84].
2. The statistical evidence to support this assertion is given elsewhere [135, 152].
3. His basic ideas are discussed in *The Entropy Law and The Economic Process* [71]. For a less technical presentation, see the opening essay of *Energy and Economic Myths* [70]. A brief summary of his system of thought is given in Chapter 7.
4. See, for example, the generally critical analysis by Levitan [124] and the negative comments by Newman [166, pp. 23–24].
5. For limited evidence on this score, see Miernyk [148].
6. After the development corridors were virtually assured of completion, the ARC shifted its emphasis to investment in facilities for the delivery of health care services and vocational education.
7. For further discussion, see Borts [20].
8. There was also an effort to redefine unemployment in ways which would benefit older industrial areas because local unemployment rates are the critical variable in formulas for the allocation of federal funds appropriated for a variety of countercyclical programs.
9. The original order was broadened under Executive Order 11731 (July 23, 1973) and Executive Order 11982 (December 31, 1975) to include "coordination of direct federal program assistance to state and local governments . . . [and to increase] the membership of the Federal Regional Councils."
10. The proposal for a stronger and more flexible regional office in Washington as a replacement for the Title V Commissions is discussed more fully in the following chapter.

Chapter 5

Regional Policy in a Nearly
Stationary State

WHAT IS A NEARLY STATIONARY
STATE?

If one uses an unfamiliar expression in a title, one is obliged to define it. What is a nearly stationary state? It is one, quite simply, that has exhibited a pronounced decline in the rate of growth of *real* output per capita or, better still, in the rate of growth of real output per employed person. Does this definition apply to the United States? It clearly does. The 1980 *Economic Report of the President* [208, p. 85] shows that GNP per employed worker grew at an annual rate of 1.9 percent from 1963 to 1973, and at an annual rate of 0.1 percent from 1973 to 1979. The "doubling time" of GNP per employed worker during the 1960s was approximately 37 years; it had lengthened to 700 years during the 1970s.

The decline of economic growth is not a uniquely American phenomenon. There have been similar declines in other industrialized nations [208]. In the sample of seven industrialized countries listed in the President's *Economic Report*, however, only one other—the United Kingdom—would qualify as a nearly stationary state.

The decline of real economic growth in the United States has been discussed in considerable detail in Edward Denison's recent *Account-*

ing for Slower Economic Growth: The United States in the 1970s [48].
Richard Stone, one of the pioneers of national income accounting, has
provided a thoughtful commentary on Denison's excellent study [204].

In the methodical manner that has become a hallmark of his
"growth accounting," Denison has analyzed the forces that have affected the efficiency of factor inputs. The sources identified account for
one-third of the decline in national income per person employed
(NIPPE). What is striking about Denison's latest analysis, however, is
that two-thirds of the change remains "unexplained"; i.e., it is a
statistical residual.

In his final chapter [48, pp. 122–147], Denison briefly discusses 17
potential causes of the unexplained portion of the decline in output per
unit of input. But he rejects some, is skeptical about others, and
concludes that "no single hypothesis seems to provide a probable
explanation of the sharp change after 1973" (p. 145).

Stone wonders if a residual is "really necessary." He suspects that to
some extent the problem is on the output side; as currently estimated,
the GNP does not include the results of "do-it-yourself" activities.
Stone also suggests that part of the decline might reflect the desire of
workers to substitute leisure for income. Primarily, however, be believes it is a matter of inadequate measurement. Stone praises Denison
for his craftsmanship, and for the diligent scholarship that keeps him
"whittling away" at the residual. But he concludes that more and
better data would provide a reasonable explanation for the unusually
large residual [204, pp. 1539–1543]. (A more convincing explanation of
the residual is offered later in this chapter.)

One other definitional matter should be cleared up at this point. The
nearly stationary state, or NSS, should not be confused with Herman
Daly's concept of the stationary state economy (SSE) [45, pp. 149–174;
44, pp. 67–94]. Space considerations preclude a complete description of
Daly's concept of the stationary state economy here. But there are two
characteristics common to both the NSS and the SSE: macro-stability
and micro-flexibility. The national economy, for example, has become
nearly stagnant, but at the same time there has been a great deal of
change in the spatial distribution of population and economic activity
(see Kones [194]).

PUBLIC POLICY AND REGIONAL SHIFTS
IN POPULATION AND EMPLOYMENT

This chapter will not cover the causes of regional shifts in
income and employment, as these have been discussed extensively
elsewhere [135, 140, 152]. Rather, this chapter is concerned with the
policy consequences of these shifts.

During the 1970s—largely as a result of the rapid, and geographically uneven, rise in energy prices—there was a fundamental change in what is loosely called the "regional problem" in this country. The problem is no longer one of "disadvantaged" regions, such as Appalachia, which failed to share in the nation's earlier robust economic growth. It has become, quite simply, a zero-sum problem of how the product of a nearly stationary state is distributed among regions. The new problem has received more attention from the popular press than it has in scholarly journals. Economists—and many regional scientists—seem more interested in retreating to less hazardous havens where they can play trivial logical games with abstract mathematical models, or to construct increasingly complex interregional systems that are "implemented" with data of dubious parentage, than in dealing with serious policy issues.

A typical journalistic reaction to the "new" regional problem is given in a somewhat emotional article by Neil Peirce [171], who has been involved with others in some solid analytical work published in the *National Journal* [91]. A report by the President's Commission on a National Agenda for the 1980s, unpublished at the time this paper was written, set Peirce off. He had access to part of this report before writing a long piece for the *Washington Post* with the value-laden title "Offing the Frost Belt: A Stupid Idea Whose Time Has Come" [171].[1] Peirce understands the zero-sum nature of the problem. He attributes the proposed "solution," however, to malevolence or political ineptitude. The commission's agenda proposed that the federal government do nothing to stem demographic and economic shifts from older industrial areas to the western and southwestern states that continue to grow. Instead, the commission recommended that the federal government grease the skids by helping stranded workers in declining regions move to areas with expanding job opportunities.

Peirce and other journalists might fulminate against the idea of relocation assistance on the ground that it is "grossly unfair" to older industrial states, which would, in effect, be subsidizing the growing states. But the idea of labor subsidies—including relocation allowances—is completely consistent with neoclassical regional economics. In a 1966 paper, Borts [20] proved that, under the traditional assumptions of neoclassical economic theory, subsidies to labor are preferable to capital or price subsidies.[2]

GEORGESCU-ROEGEN'S BIOECONOMIC PARADIGM

What logic lies behind the assumption that the United States has become a nearly stationary state? We have been told by the

Reagan administration that it will start the economy growing again. That was also the objective of the Carter administration. But the economy didn't grow. The growth nostrum makes as much sense as a similar prescription by a medical doctor as a "cure" for the physiological problems associated with middle age. We would all question the competence—or possibly the sanity—of a doctor who prescribes "more growth" as a cure for the ailments of middle age. But this is the general prescription offered by conventional economists as the cure for "stagflation."[3] The analogy of medical and economic prescriptions will be regarded by "right-thinking" economists as strained, if not simplistic. But is it?

The decline in economic growth, and in productivity, analyzed in meticulous detail by Denison, cannot be "explained" within the framework of traditional economics. The "Denison residual" has an explanation, but only if one is willing to step outside the constricting bounds of traditional economics to the bioeconomic paradigm of Nicholas Georgescu-Roegen [66, 68, 70, 71].

Bioeconomics, about which more is said in Chapter 7, is not a simple extension of earlier economic thought. It makes a complete break with the past. Instead of viewing the economic process in mechanistic terms, Georgescu-Roegen sees it as an extension of the evolutionary process. Economic systems are subject to the second law of thermodynamics— the entropy law—which states that the world's stock of energy is constantly being transformed from a "free" state to a "bound" state. This means that the total stock of energy available to mankind will decline steadily. But as population grows, the demand for energy will continue to increase. The principles of traditional economics tell us that there is only one outcome in this situation, namely, that there will be a steady increase in the *real* price of energy. Thus, a basic principle of bioeconomics is that economic systems, as well as firms, are subject to the classical law of diminishing returns.

Within this analytical framework, declining economic growth rates in advanced industrial economies are viewed as perfectly natural phenomena. Moreover, declining economic growth is an *irreversible* phenomenon because the entropic process works in one direction only. The inevitable outcome is a declining growth rate, first in relative terms, but eventually the system must encounter absolutely diminishing returns. This conclusion does not rule out the possibility of brief spurts of economic growth. But such spurts could be accomplished only by literally "borrowing from the future."[4]

What policy conclusions follow from this view of the economic process? Acceptance of the principles of bioeconomics leads, in a nutshell, to the conclusion that the search for perpetual economic growth as a solution to economic problems is a futile one. Instead,

economic policies should focus on conservation and an equitable distribution of the economic product, whatever that turns out to be.

A final word before turning to the regional consequences of the
nearly stationary state. There is nothing in Georgescu-Roegen's system of thought to suggest that a worldwide catastrophe is imminent.
Since the economic process is biological rather than mechanistic, it
will come to an end some day. But nowhere has Georgescu-Roegen
attempted to pinpoint the time, or even the exact way, in which this will
happen. He has simply pointed out that when one views the operation
of the economic system as a biological process, subject to the laws of
physics, it is inevitable that some day it will come to an end. My own
hypothesis is that when it does it will end—in the words of T. S.
Eliot—"not with a bang but a whimper."

REVERSAL OF INCOME TRANSFERS

What are the regional consequences of a sharp drop in the
national growth rate? The most obvious has been acceleration of the
long-term trend toward convergence of regional per capita income
[140, 153]. Neoclassical regional growth theorists say, incidentally,
that such convergence is a validation of neoclassical principles. The
presumption is that it will continue until remaining differentials have
been eliminated. At that point, neoclassical theory would say, spatial
equilibrium will have been reached. After that, the differentials will
be influenced by nothing stronger than "random" forces.

I disagree with this conclusion, and I reject the notion of a "spatial
equilibrium." I will argue instead that by the turn of the century, if not
before, some or all of the energy- and resource-based regions that have
not yet reached the U.S. average will rise above the national average
of per capita income. If this happens, of course, other regions will have
to drop below the average, by definition. These income shifts will not
be the result of massive industrial relocation (such as the past migration of textiles from the North to the South), but will represent a
continuation of recent shifts in comparative advantage [140].

Historically, regional income differentials could best be explained by
the Clark–Fisher hypothesis. Higher per capita incomes were associated with heavy dependence on manufacturing and tertiary activities.
Conversely, energy- and resource-based states had low per capita
incomes. But the historic Clark–Fisher relationships are breaking
down as a result of changes in regional comparative advantage.[5]

Prior to 1969, the industrialization of New England, the Middle
Atlantic, and the Upper Midwest was subsidized to a large extent by
cheap energy obtained from Appalachia and the Southwest. The indus-

trial regions, in effect, collected "economic rents" from the energy-producing (and raw materials–producing) regions. Now the shift is in the other direction. The states with rapidly rising *relative* per capita incomes are those that produce more energy than they consume (see Corrigan [38, 39] and Garnick [63, 64]). Although the evidence is not as clear in the case of agricultural regions, it is likely that they too will gain at the expense of industrial regions in the future [216].

NATIONAL GROWTH RATES AND REGIONAL DEVELOPMENT

Existing regional development policies are based on the implicit assumption of a continuation of robust national growth. I use the term "growth" in the old-fashioned sense of a long-term trend line with seasonal, cyclical, and random influences "eliminated." During the 1960s, when the Economic Development Administration and the Appalachian Regional Commission were established, the robust-growth hypothesis seemed to be reasonable. Those programs were based on what Richardson [187] has called "generative" growth theory. The basic postulate of this theory is that the national growth rate can be improved if the growth rates of "lagging" regions can be increased. Since the beginning of the 1970s, however, a far more plausible hypothesis is what Richardson has called "competitive" growth. This hypothesis assumes that the national growth rate is determined by exogenous forces, and that this rate is "distributed" among an economy's regions. It is a top-down theory consistent with the zero-sum situation approximated by the nearly stationary state. Existing regional policies were not designed to deal with these conditions.

ALTERNATIVE REGIONAL POLICIES IN A NEARLY STATIONARY STATE

What are the alternatives? If one is willing to accept the competitive hypothesis, as I am, there are two alternatives: One is to try to stop, or significantly slow, the demographic and economic shifts from older industrial regions to the South and the West. The other is to accept the shifts and, as the Commission on an Agenda for the 1980s suggests, ameliorate the problems of the people affected by these shifts.

The first alternative would require massive federal subsidies, including possible shifts of federal installations—such as military bases—from the South and the West to the Northeast and the Upper

Midwest (cf. Moynihan [164]). As noted earlier, neoclassical theory would argue against this alternative on efficiency grounds. But the second alternative, relocation allowances, and other labor subsidies, would be supported as the best of the alternatives available to policy makers within the bounds of neoclassical theory (Borts [20]).

The second alternative could also be justified within a bioeconomic framework as long as the shifts are from regions with above-average income to regions with below-average income. Clearly, it would be difficult to justify subsidies on equity principles after the relative income positions of the two regions had been switched.

What about the older industrial regions? Should their plight be ignored? Not at all. First, there is no reason to suspect that New England, the Middle Atlantic, and the Upper Midwest are likely to become depressed regions as a result of the relatively moderate and orderly demographic and economic shifts of the recent past. There is an enormous amount of embedded private and social overhead capital in these regions, and this (plus inertia) makes them desirable locations for many kinds of economic activities. These regions have exhibited a surprising resilience in spite of the loss of manufacturing employment and, in some cases, population. Not all manufacturing activities are vulnerable to rising energy prices, which are among the more important forces behind the shifts of the 1970s.[6] The basic structural changes that are taking place will continue to influence the southwestward drift of the economic center of gravity in the United States. These changes will continue to alter the economic and demographic map of the nation, as they have since colonial days, but they will not destroy any of its regions.

REDIRECTION OF NATIONAL POLICIES TOWARD REGIONAL CHANGE

What about the policies in effect in early 1981, and the agencies that administered them? To a large extent the EDA, and the ARC, and the Title V ("wall-to-wall") Commissions had become revenue-sharing intermediaries that funneled federal funds to specific states. The EDA has not been highly effective in doing the job it was originally supposed to do [141, 142]. And there was no need at all for the intermediate layer of government established under Title V to administer a revenue-sharing program that could be administered much more effectively in other ways. It also appeared that the ARC was to be allowed to run out, at least as presently constituted. This unique and largely successful experiment in federal–state relations has served its basic purpose (establishment of the development highways, multicounty regional planning districts, and a good start on various programs of investment in human capital). There will be no great loss if the federal nexus to the ARC is cut, provided revenue-sharing continues.

All the existing "regional development" apparatus could be replaced by a new Division of Regional Affairs in the U. S. Department of Commerce. This division would not need to be large, and it would be more an advisory body—comparable to the Council of Economic Advisers—than an operating agency. It could recommend policies—including revenue sharing and relocation allowances—that could be put into effect by Congress, if that body chose to do so, or in some cases by executive order. The policies themselves would be carried out by other agencies.

The new regional division could monitor the regional effects of national policies, and recommend changes when appropriate. It would also be useful if it could engage in continuous forecasting. It could, for example, project anticipated changes in the regional impacts of new national policies.

The federal agency proposed here would be far more flexible than those established during the 1960s. It would not be committed to any particular set of policies, including policies that might be rendered obsolete by future structural change. The basic weakness of the ARC and the EDA is that they were designed to operate under conditions of robust national growth. The available evidence supports the conclusion that we will not see those conditions again. Existing agencies were not designed to cope with the new regional problems engendered by the nearly stationary state.

NOTES

1. I am aware that journalists do not write their own headlines, so Peirce should not be unjustly stigmatized with this one.
2. Pages 205–207. See also the mathematical appendix, pp. 209–218, for Borts's proof of these propositions.
3. "Conventional economists," as I use this term, covers the spectrum from Marxists through the neoclassical and Keynesian schools to the neo-Keynesian school.
4. Georgescu-Roegen has many admirers. Relatively few economists, however, seem willing to accept his system of thought in its entirety. His ideas have had a greater impact on Western Europe and other parts of the world than in the United States. Although regional scientists are less tradition-bound than conventional economists, there is little evidence that Georgescu-Roegen's ideas are well known in this discipline.
5. On this, see Miernyk [135, 152, and esp. 140]. For evidence that the Clark–Fisher relationship is changing at the international level as well, see Kader [104].
6. For evidence to support this contention, see Miernyk 132, 140.

Chapter 6

Regional and Environmental Consequences of Rising Energy Prices

THE INTERDEPENDENCE OF ENVIRONMENTAL AND ENERGY PROBLEMS

The industrial nations of the world live from one crisis to another, and there has been a tendency for crises to overlap. The dominant crises in the United States during the past quarter-century can be cataloged fairly specifically. During the 1950s the major problem was economic stagnation. The decade of the 1960s was characterized by uninterrupted economic growth, but among the undesirable side effects were rapid increases in air, water, and solid-waste pollution. This was the decade of the environmental crisis.

Energy prices began to rise in the late 1960s as rapid increases in demand for all forms of energy exerted pressure on existing supplies. The problem was exacerbated by the OPEC oil embargo of late 1973, which led to a sudden quadrupling of world petroleum prices. Energy prices would have continued to rise without the events of September 1973, but the sudden upsurge of prices following the embargo provided a dramatic introduction to the latest of the world's crises [140, 155].

The theme of this chapter is that energy and environmental problems are interdependent. We aren't likely to "solve" either, in an equilibrium sense, but the two problems can and should be attacked simultaneously. The data used to illustrate one approach to the amelioration of these joint problems relate to the United States. But the conclusions are as applicable to any other industrial nation as they are to the United States.

Environmental economics is a new and still somewhat experimental branch of the discipline. Economists are quick to bend with the winds of change, and there is already a substantial body of literature dealing with environmental matters. Much of it is utterly useless as far as policy prescription is concerned. The application of traditional neoclassical methods to environmental problems has resulted in a long string of sterile exercises (see, e.g., Fisher and Peterson [58]). Some attempt to define Pareto-optimal levels of pollution; others discuss the internalization of externalities. But unlike the work of Leontief, Cumberland, and a few others, they do not deal with the technical (or engineering) relationships between production and environmental degradation. Traditional macroeconomic analysis, which continues to stress economic growth as a *sine qua non,* has been perhaps even more nugatory in providing policy guidance.

THE TECHNOLOGICAL OPTIMISTS

The father of modern macroeconomics, John Maynard Keynes, is remembered less for his views about economic growth than for the short-run analyses of the *General Theory.* Indeed, one of his most widely quoted assertions is that "in the long run we shall all be dead!" But Keynes's views on the long run, which predate publication of the *General Theory,* are illuminating. He was an unabashed technological optimist who felt that the economic problem was not *"the permanent problem of the human race."* Indeed, he believed that in the absence of major wars and with "no important increase in population" the *"economic problem* may be solved, or be at least within sight of solution, within a hundred years" [107, p. 366].

The essay from which these quotations are taken, "Economic Possibilities for Our Grandchildren," was written in 1930. In that context, Keynes's optimistic views are understandable. After all, the major problem that Great Britain had faced for nearly a decade was one of inadequate aggregate demand. This was to be the major problem of the United States for the decade following publication of the essay.

A contemporary American futurist—Herman Kahn—appears to accept the Keynesian vision while dropping the constraint of "no important population increases." Kahn foresees a world population of

15 billion in the year 2176 (give or take a factor of two, i.e., a *range* of 7.5 to 30 billion), and a per capita gross world product (GWP) of $20,000 [105, p. 7]. Since he says nothing about price changes, one can only assume that this projection is in 1976 prices. There is, of course, a range around the worldwide average, from $10,000 in what Kahn calls the world's "noncoping" countries (i.e., the LDCs) to $40,000 in developed countries [105, pp. 56–57].

In his long-run scenario, Keynes simply ignored resource constraints—a practice that most theoretical economists still follow. Kahn does not ignore energy and resource matters. In a chapter entitled "Exhaustible to Inexhaustible," which is fairly skimpy in terms of data, he concludes, "Except for temporary fluctuations caused by bad luck [sic] or poor management, the world need not worry about energy shortages or costs in the future. And energy abundance is probably the world's best insurance that the entire human population (even 15–20 billion) can be well cared for, at least physically, during many centuries to come" [105, pp. 33]. As for other resources—some of which are already in short supply with rising prices—Kahn cheerfully concludes, "In time, the rocks and ocean will constitute an essentially *infinite* resource base. . ." [105, p. 105]. He has "solved" the world's future energy and resource problems by invoking Disney's First Law— "Wishing Will Make It So" [155].

Kahn is equally optimistic about our ability to solve environmental problems. He concedes that mistakes and setbacks will result from "overzealous programs or excessive political pressure." But he concludes that "probably by ten or fifteen years from now, almost certainly by the year 2000, it is very likely that we will be able to look with great pride on our accomplishments. We will breathe clean air, drink directly from rivers, and enjoy pleasing landscapes" [105, p. 162]. Interestingly, Kahn is not quite so positive about the *very* long run. "It may yet turn out," he says, "that future man will marvel at the paradoxical combination of hubris and modesty of 20th century man, who, at the same time, so exaggerated his ability to do damage and so underestimated his own ability to adapt to or solve such problems. Or it could be that future man, *if he exists,* will wonder at the recklessness and callousness of 20th century scientists and governments" [105, p. 180, emphasis added].

Kahn treats energy and environmental problems separately. By contrast, the ecologist Barry Commoner stresses interdependence between economic and ecosystems [37].[1] He makes the blunt assertion that "pollution control reduces energy supplies; energy conservation costs jobs" [37].

It is true that in special circumstances pollution control *can* reduce energy supplies. If energy is used to power precipitators, for example, that energy cannot be used for the production of goods.[2] It does not follow, however, that every type of pollution control will lead to the increased use of energy, and hence impose a further drain on limited energy supplies. Similarly, energy conservation need not cost jobs. One way to conserve energy is to shift from capital-intensive to labor-intensive production processes. That would be a departure from the historical trend of searching for increasingly capital-intensive (and energy-intensive) production processes, but it most assuredly is one way to conserve energy and to increase employment at the same time.

Commoner has little use for fossil fuels or nuclear energy. Solar energy is for him the desideratum. He is realistic enough to know that it will be a long time coming, but he is clear on the ordering of his priorities. "When the facts are known," he says, "it turns out that solar energy cannot only replace a good deal, and eventually all, of the present consumption of conventional fuels—and eliminate that much environmental pollution—but can also *reverse the trend* toward escalating energy costs that is so seriously affecting the economic system" [37, p. 122]. This is the kind of assertion that no doubt led Passell to make his recommendation that readers ignore Commoner's economic pronouncements.

One of the consequences of the "energy crisis" in the United States has been extensive examination of the ways in which we waste energy. Commoner estimates the overall efficiency of energy use in the United States at about 15 percent. Industry comes off with a slightly better rating—about 25 to 30 percent. Thus Commoner (and many others) believes that an enormous amount of energy can be saved simply by increasing the efficiency of its use (see Stobaugh and Yergin [203]). This inefficiency, it should be pointed out, is not due to either sloth or stupidity, but to the present state of the engineering arts, and to economic costs. We do not strive to use energy in the most efficient way, but in the most profitable way. The two are not necessarily the same.

Commoner's entry into the burgeoning list of studies of energy and environmental problems in the United States contains much that is useful, although it includes no new facts. His discussion of the second law of thermodynamics—hailed by reviewers for the clarity of its exposition—suffers by comparison with that of Georgescu-Roegen [69]. Georgescu's discussion of the entropy law is more rigorous than Commoner's, and equally understandable to laymen. But the strangest thing about Commoner's book is that it fails to reach a conclusion. Toward the end, Commoner becomes involved in a confused and confusing discussion of the declining rate of "profit." He goes on to say:

Here we come to the end of the blind, mindless chain of events that transformed the technologies of agricultural and industrial production and reorganized transportation; that increased the output of the production system, but increased even more its appetite for capital, energy, and other resources; that eliminated jobs and degraded environment; that concentrated the physical power of energy and the social power of the resultant wealth into ever fewer, larger corporations; that has fed this power on a diet of unemployment and poverty. *Here is the basic fault* that has spawned the environmental crisis and the energy crisis, and that threatens—if no remedy is found—to engulf us in the wreckage of a crumbling economic system. [37, p. 264, emphasis added]

Nowhere does Commoner make the meaning of this "basic fault" clear, but evidently it is the economic system. Moreover, it is far from evident that Commoner understands this system, or even that he understands the elementary market forces that have caused the rise in energy prices throughout the world. This should surprise no one, of course, since Commoner is not a trained economist. What is surprising, given his eminence in the scientific community, is his implicit belief that energy and environmental problems are entirely the result of imperfect economic and political institutions. Despite his extended discussion of the entropy law, he fails to make the fundamental connection between entropy and the world's energy supply.

I am not suggesting that the political, economic, and social institutions of the United States are without fault. What I am suggesting—or rather, stating explicitly—is that elimination of the profit motive (if that could be achieved), or even the elimination of individual greed and avarice, would not solve the world's energy and environmental problems. Even in an ideal communal society, tradeoffs would have to be made.

Those who have an absolute faith that technology will solve mankind's problems are extrapolating long-run trends. But the quantum jump in gross output per capita in the world's developed nations during the past century—and more particularly during the past twenty-five years—can be explained basically by rapid technological development and *cheap energy*. The latter is something the world will not see again.

REGIONAL IMPACTS OF RISING ENERGY PRICES

In this chapter I will only summarize the results of work on the regional impacts of rising energy prices reported more fully elsewhere

[140, 155]. Low-cost energy subsidized urbanization and contributed heavily to improved methods of agricultural production in the United States. Impressive gains in productivity—the result of mechanization, and of major improvements in chemical technology—permitted a rapidly declining number of farmers to provide food and fiber for a growing population [214, p. 40]. Indeed, from the early 1920s until the late 1960s, the "long-run" agricultural problem was one of chronic surpluses. We are not likely to see such surpluses again. There will be further technological improvements in agriculture, but a major constraint on productivity gains in the future will be the limited availability of energy.

Cheap energy was the result of aggressive price competition both within and between fuels when supplies were relatively abundant. While consumers benefited from this competition, returns to the factors of production—particularly labor—remained low. Thus, energy-producing regions in the United States, and to a large extent elsewhere in the world, tended to be relatively poor. In the United States, for example, the Appalachian region was until recently the major supplier of coal to the nation, as well as to foreign buyers. But when the nation moved into the "Age of Affluence" following World War II, Appalachia remained a severely depressed region.

The world depends primarily on fossil fuels—coal, petroleum, and natural gas—for most of its energy. And the prices of fossil fuels are no longer determined in competitive markets. The rise of OPEC is a story too well known to be repeated here. Perhaps less well known is the movement that resulted in the merger of a number of large coal and petroleum companies in the United States. It is an open secret that the prices of all basic fuels are now administered rather than determined by open market forces.

This does not mean that the energy problem can be solved by dissolution of the corporate energy giants. Such a move would have no effect on the international petroleum cartel, and as long as this cartel survives, world petroleum prices will be administered rather than competitively determined. With an international umbrella over petroleum prices, it is not likely that domestic energy prices can be reduced by administrative fiat. Energy prices are high and rising not only because of new institutional arrangements, but primarily because the world's supply of fossil fuels is dwindling relative to demand. Thus energy prices will continue to rise faster than other prices. This does not portend a collapse of the world economy, but it does mean that there will have to be continued adjustments.

One adjustment that has already started in the United States is a shift of real income from energy-consuming to energy-producing regions. Per capita income is rising more rapidly than the national average in energy-producing states, while the reverse is true in some of the nation's older industrial states. In the latter, while per capita income remains well above the national average, increases have been relatively small.

Another indicator of the shift in relative well-being between energy-producing and energy-consuming states is to be found in public finance. Many of the older industrial states—and virtually all major cities in the United States—have experienced budgetary difficulties in recent years. Meanwhile, the nation's energy-producing states—and some of its major agricultural producers—have experienced budget surpluses.

Changes in underlying economic conditions have started a slow migration from the industrial Northeast to southern and western regions, where fossil fuels are available at lower delivered prices. Within the next two decades, there could be a substantial rearrangement of industry and population in the United States. This is the period during which the nation will rely increasingly on fossil fuels—particularly coal—and during which regions with large stocks of fossil fuels should experience growth while other regions will experience relative or, in some cases, absolute decline. Since energy-consuming regions are at present relatively high-income regions and energy producers are relatively low-income regions, there will be increased convergence in real per capita income between these regions. This significant change in the relative income position of regions in the United States is discussed more fully in the following chapter.

ENERGY NONUSE AS ANTIPOLLUTION POLICY

As Leontief pointed out in a paper first delivered in Tokyo in 1970 [114], pollution may be handled analytically just as any other "output" of the economic system. Since pollution is, to some extent, a function of energy inputs, one way to attack environmental and energy problems simultaneously would be to reduce the consumption of energy, which would automatically reduce pollution.

There is a growing recognition in the United States that the only way to stretch energy supplies in the short run is to conserve effectively (see, for example, Berg [16]; Lincoln [126]; and Stobaugh and Yergin [203]). But conventional conservation proposals emphasize the savings in energy that would result from greater efficiency in its use. While any development that would result in *net* savings in energy should be welcomed, increased efficiency in energy use might not be sufficient to have major impacts on either energy or environmental problems.

There is a small, but evidently a growing, movement in the United States that seeks to go beyond conventional conservation measures in pursuit of a policy of energy *nonuse*. One of the leading advocates of this policy is Rustum Roy of Pennsylvania State University, who has argued that "if the country is prepared to spend hundreds of millions of dollars on each of geothermal and solar energy, to say nothing of billions for fusion and LMSBRs, not one of which has the potential of NOU-energy [his acronym for nonuse of energy], it is not unreasonable to put equivalent sums into energy education *for this purpose*" [195, p. 2]. In the same vein, Congresswoman Mink of Hawaii introduced a bill entitled the "Energy-Materials Conservation Education Act of 1975," which, had it been enacted, would have provided grants for special educational programs and activities "designed to achieve conservation and nonuse of energy and materials. . ." [211, p. 1].

The need for such an educational program has been highlighted by a survey that showed that the American public does not know what to believe about the energy supply problem. Since Americans have been exposed to a variety of contradictory statements, they do not know what to believe about the available supply of energy (for further details, see Thompson and MacTavish [205]).

SECTORAL EFFECTS OF NONUSE: AN ILLUSTRATIVE EXAMPLE

The effects of a policy of nonuse can be illustrated by the 1967 U.S. Input–Output Table.[3] For purposes of this illustration, the coal, crude petroleum, and natural gas sectors were combined with electrical utilities into a single "energy sector."[4] Whether entirely justified or not, we assume for purposes of this exercise that air pollution from stationary sources is a linear, homogeneous function of energy consumption.[5] Pollution coefficients were calculated for each sector from emissions data from the 1970 Annual Report of the Council of Environmental Quality.[6] These coefficients are smaller than those calculated by Leontief and Ford using 1963 data [119]. I suspect their coefficients are more realistic, but it was necessary to calculate original coefficients for this study because of the definition of a separate energy sector.

Since a linear relationship between energy consumption and pollution output was postulated, the largest consumers of energy (per dollar of output) are also the largest direct *and indirect* producers of pollution (per dollar of output).[7] There are some surprises in this list, which includes such activities as trade, real estate, and medical and educational services, as well as state and local government enterprises. These are usually not thought of as major polluters because their contribution to pollution is *indirect,* via their consumption of electrical energy.

How much energy would the nation have saved, and how much would pollution from stationary sources have been abated in 1967, if the final sales of each of the ten largest energy consumers had been reduced 10 percent by a successful nonuse program? Because of the importance of these sectors to the economy, such cuts would have led to a reduction in total final demand of almost $35 billion, in 1967 dollars, or almost 4.6 percent. But the appropriate impact to measure is the effect that changes of this magnitude would have had on total gross output. Here the cutback would have amounted to $64 billion, or 4.5 percent.

Before the simulated cutback, the nation's intermediate or processing sectors generated 88.3 million tons of pollutants (final consumers contributed an additional 35.4 million). The 4.6-percent reduction in final sales would have reduced emissions by a modest 6.4 million tons, or 7.3 percent.

As expected, the largest changes in total gross output—and hence in pollution—are found in sectors with significant sales to final consumers. The largest are the energy and petroleum-refining sectors. Others, such as primary metals, which sell most of their output to intermediate purchasers, registered small changes in output and pollution abatement. Thus a truly effective policy of energy nonuse and pollution abatement would have to be based on a set of criteria for reducing energy inputs rather than the single criterion of reduced sales to find demand. The latter was chosen in the present exercise purely for analytical convenience. A significant finding, even in this simulated exercise, is that a reduction in energy consumption would have a large impact on service sectors as well as on those producing goods. This, of course, is simply a result of the interdependence of economic activities, a feature of real economic life that is captured by input–output tables.

But wouldn't a policy with effects such as those described mean that we would be going backwards? How can these results be squared with the unmitigated optimism of Kahn and others who believe that technology will, as in the past, lead to an ever-increasing standard of living throughout the world? The answer is that they cannot. Technological optimists believe that energy will be available in abundance and at low prices. The proposal of a policy of nonuse is based on an opposite view. It involves the explicit recognition that, given the present state of technology, we cannot conserve energy *and* reduce pollution while expanding output. Unfortunately, that appears to be the objective of most policy proposals made in the United States.[8]

There almost certainly will be new technical developments that will increase the efficiency of energy use. The development of gas turbines on a broad scale would be a major step in this direction. And in a country such as the United States there is a great deal of room for the reduction of palpable waste. These are the goals of the conventional conservationists whose prosaic prescriptions, such as better home insulation, are already being implemented. Conservation measures will of course be necessary if the developed nations of the world are to achieve the twin goals of stretching available energy supplies and improving the environment, but they will not be sufficient. Only a determined, successful program of nonuse can accomplish this end.

Is this really what the people of the developed nations want? That is the question raised by those who ask what posterity has done for us. Wanted or not, however, some of these effects are likely to be realized during the next quarter-century, and possibly for a much longer period. Dwindling energy supplies and increasing entropy will virtually guarantee a reduction in the consumption of energy on a per capita basis in the United States, and probably in other advanced countries. The LDCs (Kahn's "noncoping" countries) will undoubtedly make energy conservation a central tenet of their development programs. There is no way that they can hope to replicate the rapid expansion of industrial production that was accomplished in the developed nations during the era of cheap energy.

For the developed nations a reduction in per capita energy consumption will dictate changes in lifestyle. Instead of a constant search for more capital- and energy-intensive activities, and a constantly expanding gross national product per capita, we will be forced by market forces—coupled with increasing demand for *effective* full-employment policies—to revert to more labor-intensive production methods. This is the essence of Schumacher's proposals in *Small Is Beautiful* [198].

It is still chic in some academic circles to denigrate Schumacher's work by calling it "pop economics." But his might turn out to be the most sensible policy proposal of our generation. As he has shown, the kind of economy he advocates is consistent with Eastern philosophies and religious views. Rustum Roy has similarly argued that a policy of energy nonuse "can be unambiguously connected to Christian ethics via the imperative to share" [196]. Most modern economists—especially those who have succumbed to the scientism of mathematical model building—will not be much impressed by these views. But it might be worth pondering the words of Lord Keynes on the same theme:

> When the accumulation of wealth is no longer of high social importance, there will be great changes in the code of morals. We shall be able to rid ourselves of many of the pseudo-moral principles which have hag-ridden us for two hundred years, by which we have exalted some of the most distasteful of human qualities into the position of highest virtues. We shall be able to afford to dare to assess the money-motive and its true value. The love of money as a possession—as distinguished from love of money as a means of the enjoyments and realities of life—will be recognized for what it is, a somewhat disgusting morbidity, one of those semi-terminal, semi-pathological propensities which one hands over with a shudder to the specialists in mental disease. All kinds of social customs and economic practices, affecting the distribution of wealth and of economic rewards and penalties, which we now maintain at all cost . . . we shall then be free, at last, to discard.

In a later passage he says:

> I see us free, therefore, to return to some of the most sure and certain principles of religion and traditional virtue—that avarice is a vice, that the exaction of usury is a misdemeanour, and the love of money is detestable, that those walk most truly in the paths of virtue and sane wisdom who take least thought for the morrow. We shall once more value ends above means and prefer the good to the useful. We shall honour those who can teach us how to pluck the hour and the day virtuously and well, the delightful people who are capable of taking direct enjoyment in things, the lilies of the field who toil not, neither do they spin. [107, pp. 369–372]

Keynes was talking, of course, about a world such as that envisaged by Kahn in 2176, in which most economic desires have been essentially sated, and in which there would be no further need for the pursuit of wealth.[9] The kind of world that Keynes has described is entirely consistent, however, with one in which there has been a conscious decision—democratically achieved—to strive for a more equitable distribution of what we are able to produce with a dwindling stock of free (as opposed to bound) energy in an environment that would be far from pristine but cleaner than the one we know today.

Table 6–1. Changes in U.S. Total Gross Output Resulting from 10-Percent Reduction in Sales to Final Demand by Selected Sectors*

	Total Gross Output (millions of 1967 $)		Changes in TGO	
Sector	Original[a]	Adjusted[b]	Dollars	Percentage
1. Livestock & livestock prods.	30,638	28,038	−2,600	−8.49
2. Other agricultural prods.	28,540	26,954	−1,586	−5.56
3. Forestry & fishery prods.	1,945	1,891	−54	−2.77
4. Agric., forestry, & fishery svcs.	2,670	2,517	−153	−5.74
5. Iron & ferroalloy ores mining	1,744	1,712	−32	−1.83
6. Nonferrous metal ores mining	1,640	1,621	−19	−1.16
* 7. Energy	37,892	32,753	−5,139	−13.56
8. Store & clay mining & quarrying	2,355	2,307	−48	−2.03
9. Chem. & fertil. mineral mining	1,027	990	−37	−3.61
10. New construction	79,889	79,889	0	0.0
11. Maintenance & repair constr.	23,391	22,132	−1,259	−5.38
12. Ordnance & accessories	10,733	10,725	−8	−0.07
*13. Food & kindred prods.	89,451	80,720	−8,731	−9.76
14. Tobacco manufactures	7,940	7,938	−2	−0.03
15. Broad & narrow fabrics	15,966	15,886	−80	−0.50
16. Misc. textile goods & floor covg.	4,668	4,628	−40	−0.86
17. Apparel	22,566	22,525	−41	−0.18
18. Misc. fabricated textile prods.	4,283	4,253	−30	−0.69
19. Lumber & wood prods., except containers	12,905	12,770	−135	−1.05
20. Wooc containers	543	514	−29	−5.25
21. Household furniture	5,122	5,116	−6	−0.12
22. Other furniture & fixtures	2,822	2,817	−5	−0.17
23. Paper & allied prods., except containers	16,733	16,198	−535	−3.20
24. Paperboard containers & boxes	6,031	5,742	−289	−4.79
25. Printing & publishing	22,118	21,512	−606	−2.74
*26. Chemicals & chemical prods.	23,182	22,032	−1,150	−4.96
27. Plastic & synthetic materials	8,424	8,287	−137	−1.63
28. Drugs, cleaning, & toilet preps.	12,582	12,361	−221	−1.76
29. Paints & allied prods.	2,914	2,836	−78	−2.69
*30. Petrol. refining & related prods.	26,975	25,012	−1,963	−7.28
31. Rubber & misc. plastic prods.	13,809	13,520	−289	−2.09
32. Leather tanning & leather prods.	1,090	1,087	−3	−0.31
33. Footwear & other leather prods.	4,240	4,232	−8	−0.19
34. Glass & glass prods.	3,801	3,661	−140	−3.68
35. Stone & clay prods.	11,026	10,911	−115	−1.04
*36. Primary ron & steel mfg.	31,723	31,146	−577	−1.82
	20,670	20,670	−200	−0.96

86

38.	Metal containers	3,355	3,112	-243	-7.23
39.	Heating, plumbing, & metal prods.	12,510	12,403	-107	-0.86
40.	Stampings, screw machine prods.	9,293	9,187	-106	-1.14
41.	Other fabricated metal prods.	12,519	12,355	-164	-1.31
42.	Engines & turbines	3,825	3,799	-26	-0.68
43.	Farm machinery & equip.	4,826	4,799	-27	-0.57
44.	Constr., mining, & oil field mach.	5,974	5,922	-52	-0.87
45.	Materials handling mach. & equip.	2,538	2,518	-20	-0.78
46.	Metalworking mach. & equip.	8,676	8,622	-54	-0.62
47.	Spec. industry mach. & equip.	5,681	5,630	-51	-0.89
48.	Gen. industrial mach.	7,800	7,719	-81	-1.03
49.	Machine shop prods.	3,940	3,888	-52	-1.32
50.	Office, computing, & acctg. mach.	6,682	6,640	-42	-0.62
51.	Service industry machines	5,279	5,248	-31	-0.58
52.	Elect. ind. equip. & apparatus	9,903	9,822	-81	-0.82
53.	Household appliances	5,450	5,426	-24	-0.45
54.	Elect. lighting & wiring equip.	4,118	4,073	-45	-1.09
55.	Radio, TV, & commun. equip.	17,331	17,298	-33	-0.19
56.	Electronic comp. & accessories	8,147	8,109	-38	-0.47
57.	Misc. elect. machinery & equip.	3,136	3,108	-28	-0.89
58.	Motor vehicles & equip.	43,740	43,650	-90	-0.21
59.	Aircraft & parts	21,993	21,965	-28	-0.13
60.	Other transportation equip.	7,811	7,791	-20	-0.25
61.	Scientific & controlling instruments	6,191	6,130	-61	-0.99
62.	Optical, ophthalmic, & photo equip.	4,779	4,747	-52	-1.10
63.	Misc. manufacturing	9,357	9,272	-85	-0.91
64.	Transportation & warehousing	52,825	51,708	-1,117	-2.12
65.	Communication, except radio & TV	19,328	18,925	-403	-2.08
66.	Radio & TV broadcasting	3,183	3,064	-119	-3.75
*67.	Gas, water, & sanitary svcs.	17,623	16,072	-1,551	-8.80
*68.	Wholesale & retail trade	163,365	149,671	-13,594	-8.38
69.	Finance & insurance	47,711	46,754	-957	-2.01
*70.	Real estate & rental	113,253	103,521	-9,732	-8.59
71.	Hotels, personal & repair svcs.	20,805	20,644	-161	-0.77
72.	Business services	56,444	54,359	-2,085	-3.69
73.	Automobile repair & svcs.	14,756	14,454	-302	-2.05
74.	Amusement	6,644	9,551	-93	-0.96
*75.	Medical, educ. svcs., & nonprofit org.	48,507	43,776	-4,731	-9.75
76.	Federal govt. enterprises	7,691	7,321	-370	-4.81
*77.	State & local govt. enterprises	9,647	8,798	-849	-8.80
		1,413,884	1,349,728	-64,156	-4.54

aSurvey of Current Business (February 1974) [217], p. 43.
bFollowing 10-percent reduction in final sales by sectors marked with *.

87

Table 6–2. U.S. Energy Input and Pollution Coefficients, 1967

Sector	Direct Energy Raw Coefficients [a]	Pollution Coefficients [b]
1. Livestock & livestock prods.	0.00231	0.00934
2. Other agricultural prods.	0.00172	0.00744
3. Forestry & fishery prods.	0.00001	0.00033
4. Agric., forestry, & fishery svcs.	0.00004	0.00170
5. Iron & ferroalloy ores mining	0.00085	0.06010
6. Nonferrous metal ores mining	0.00099	0.07446
7. Energy	0.08213	0.26812
8. Stone & clay mining & quarrying	0.00164	0.08596
9. Chem . & fertil. mineral mining	0.00057	0.06833
10. New construction	0.00105	0.00163
11. Maintenance & repair constr.	0.00016	0.00085
12. Ordnance & accessories	0.00110	0.01273
13. Food & kindred prods.	0.01053	0.01456
14. Tobacco manufactures	0.00026	0.00411
15. Broad & narrow fabrics	0.00402	0.03118
16. Misc. textile goods & floor covg.	0.00065	0.01730
17. Apparel	0.00202	0.01110
18. Misc. fabricated textile prods.	0.00044	0.01273
19. Lumber & wood prods., except containers	0.00248	0.02377
20. Wood containers	0.00010	0.02164
21. Household furniture	0.00070	0.01701
22. Other furniture & fixtures	0.00036	0.01560
23. Paper & allied prods., except containers	0.00661	0.04884
24. Paperboard containers & boxes	0.00083	0.01701
25. Printing & publishing	0.00155	0.00865
26. Chemicals & chemical prods.	0.01257	0.06709
27. Plastic & synthetic materials	0.00278	0.04077
28. Drugs, cleaning, & toilet preps.	0.00100	0.00983
29. Paints & allied prods.	0.00026	0.01120
30. Petrol. refining & related prods.	0.30905	0.41723
31. Rubber & misc. plastic prods.	0.00335	0.03000
32. Leather tanning & leather prods.	0.00020	0.02246
33. Footwear & other leather prods.	0.00040	0.01175
34. Glass & glass prods.	0.00118	0.03829
35. Stone & clay prods.	0.00590	0.06620
36. Primary iron & steel mfg.	0.02833	0.11047
37. Primary nonferrous metal mfg.	0.00749	0.04440
38. Metal containers	0.00036	0.01342

88

		a	b
39.	Heating, plumbing, & metal prods.	0.00156	0.01541
40.	Stampings, screw machine prods.	0.00162	0.02161
41.	Other fabricated metal prods.	0.00217	0.02142
42.	Engines & turbines	0.00039	0.01273
43.	Farm machinery & equip.	0.00031	0.00790
44.	Constr., mining, & oil field mach.	0.00076	0.01583
45.	Materials handling mach. & equip.	0.00022	0.01094
46.	Metalworking mach. & equip.	0.00110	0.01564
47.	Spec. industry mach. & equip.	0.00060	0.01306
48.	Gen. industrial mach.	0.00098	0.01560
49.	Machine shop prods.	0.00078	0.02439
50.	Office, computing, & acctg. mach.	0.00042	0.00780
51.	Service industry machines	0.00048	0.01126
52.	Elect. ind. equip. & apparatus	0.00140	0.01747
53.	Household appliances	0.00081	0.01831
54.	Elect. lighting & wiring equip.	0.00070	0.02109
55.	Radio, TV, & commun. equip.	0.00163	0.01162
56.	Electronic comp. & accessories	0.00127	0.01933
57.	Misc. elect. machinery & equip.	0.00039	0.01531
58.	Motor vehicles & equip.	0.00391	0.01107
59.	Aircraft & parts	0.00151	0.00849
60.	Other transportation equip.	0.00090	0.01423
61.	Scientific & controlling instruments	0.00061	0.01221
62.	Optical, ophthalmic, & photo equip.	0.00040	0.01045
63.	Misc. manufacturing	0.00109	0.01440
64.	Transportation & warehousing	0.00613	0.01436
65.	Communication, except radio & TV	0.00248	0.01590
66.	Radio & TV broadcasting	0.00088	0.03434
67.	Gas, water, & sanitary svcs.	0.05935	0.41659
68.	Wholesale & retail trade	0.04163	0.03493
69.	Finance & insurance	0.00657	0.01704
70.	Real estate & rental	0.01019	0.01113
71.	Hotels, personal & repair svcs.	0.00658	0.03914
72.	Business services	0.00209	0.00457
73.	Automobile repair & svcs.	0.00189	0.01587
74.	Amusement	0.00162	0.02076
75.	Medical, educ. svcs., & nonprofit org.	0.01868	0.04763
76.	Federal govt. enterprises	0.00441	0.07094
77.	State & local govt. enterprises	0.02512	0.32214

a Purchases from energy sector in cents per dollar of output.
b Thousands of tons of pollutants per million dollars of output.

Table 6–3. Stationary Sources and Effects of Hypothesized Changes in U.S. Sales to Final Demand

Sector	Sources of Pollution (thousands of tons)		Changes in Pollution	
	Original	Adjusted	Thousands of Tons	Percentage
1. Livestock & livestock prods.	286.05	261.78	–24.28	–8.49
2. Other agricultural prods.	212.43	200.62	–11.81	–5.56
3. Forestry & fishery prods.	0.63	0.62	–0.02	–2.77
4. Ag'ic., forestry, & fishery svcs.	4.53	4.27	–0.26	–5.74
5. Iron & ferroalloy ores mining	104.81	102.90	–1.91	–1.83
6. Nonferrous metal ores mining	122.12	120.70	–1.42	–1.16
7. Energy	10,159.46	8,781.63	–1,377.83	–13.56
8. Stone & clay mining & quarrying	202.42	198.32	–4.10	–2.03
9. Chem. & fertil. mineral mining	70.17	67.64	–2.53	–3.61
10. New construction	130.40	130.40	0.0	0.0
11. Maintenance & repair constr.	19.85	18.79	–1.07	–5.38
12. Ordnance & accessories	136.65	136.55	–0.10	–0.07
13. Food & kindred prods.	1,302.39	1,175.28	–127.12	–9.76
14. Tobacco manufactures	32.66	32.65	–0.01	–0.03
15. Broad & narrow fabrics	497.76	495.27	–2.49	–0.50
16. Misc. textile goods & floor covg.	80.77	80.07	–0.70	–0.86
17. Apparel	250.47	250.02	–0.45	–0.18
18. Misc. fabricated textile prods.	54.53	54.15	–0.38	–0.69
19. Lumber & wood prods., except containers	306.70	303.48	–3.22	–1.05
20. Wood containers	11.75	11.14	–0.62	–5.25
21. Household furniture	87.12	87.02	–0.10	–0.12
22. Other furniture & fixtures	44.04	43.96	–0.07	–0.17
23. Paper & allied prods., except containers	817.20	791.06	–26.14	–3.20
24. Pape-board containers & boxes	102.58	97.67	–4.91	–4.79
25. Printing & publishing	191.34	186.10	–5.24	–2.74
26. Chemicals & chemical prods.	1,555.19	1,478.04	–77.16	–4.96
27. Plastic & synthetic materials	343.48	337.88	–5.60	–1.63
28. Drugs, cleaning, & toilet preps.	123.63	121.46	–2.17	–1.76
29. Paints & allied prods.	32.63	31.45	–0.88	–2.69
30. Petrol. refining & related inds.	38,229.90	35,447.33	–2,782.57	–7.28
31. Rubber & misc. plastic prods.	414.20	405.62	–8.67	–2.09
32. Leather tanning & leather prods.	24.48	24.41	–0.07	–0.31
33. Footwear & other leather prods.	49.83	49.74	–0.09	–0.19
34. Glass & glass prods.	145.55	140.19	–5.36	–3.68
35. Stone & clay prods.	729.97	722.35	–7.63	–1.04
36. Primary iron & steel mfg.	3,504.50	3,440.72	–63.78	–1.82
37. Primary nonferrous metal mfg.	926.58	917.72	–8.86	–0.96

38.	Metal containers	45.01	41.76	-3.26	-7.23
39.	Heating, plumbing, & metal prods.	192.76	191.11	-1.66	-0.86
40.	Stampings, screw machine prods.	200.83	198.54	-2.29	-1.14
41.	Other fabricated metal prods.	268.10	264.59	-3.51	-1.31
42.	Engines & turbines	48.70	48.37	-0.33	-0.68
43.	Farm machinery & equip.	38.13	37.91	-0.22	-0.57
44.	Constr., mining, & oil field mach.	94.59	93.77	-0.82	-0.87
45.	Materials handling mach. & equip.	27.76	27.54	-0.22	-0.78
46.	Metalworking mach. & equip.	135.67	134.83	-0.84	-0.62
47.	Spec. industry mach. & equip.	74.18	73.52	-0.66	-0.89
48.	Gen. industrial mach.	121.72	120.46	-1.26	-1.03
49.	Machine shop prods.	96.08	94.82	-1.26	-1.32
50.	Office, computing, & acctg. mach.	52.13	51.81	-0.32	-0.62
51.	Service industry machines	59.46	59.11	-0.34	-0.58
52.	Elect. ind. equip. & apparatus	172.96	171.54	-1.42	-0.82
53.	Household appliances	99.81	99.37	-0.44	-0.45
54.	Elect. lighting & wiring equip.	86.84	85.90	-0.94	-1.09
55.	Radio, TV, & commun. equip.	201.42	201.03	-0.38	-0.19
56.	Electronic comp. & accessories	157.45	156.71	-0.74	-0.47
57.	Misc. elect. machinery & equip.	48.01	47.59	-0.43	-0.89
58.	Motor vehicles & equip.	484.06	483.06	-1.00	-0.21
59.	Aircraft & parts	186.67	186.43	-0.24	-0.13
60.	Other transportation equip.	111.18	110.90	-0.28	-0.25
61.	Scientific & controlling instruments	75.59	74.84	-0.75	-0.99
62.	Optical, ophthalmic, & photo equip.	49.92	49.38	-0.55	-1.10
63.	Misc. manufacturing	134.71	133.49	-1.22	-0.91
64.	Transportation & warehousing	758.78	742.73	-16.05	-2.12
65.	Communication, except radio & TV	307.28	300.88	-6.40	-2.08
66.	Radio & TV broadcasting	109.31	105.21	-4.10	-3.75
67.	Gas, water, & sanitary svcs.	7,341.52	6,695.24	-646.29	-8.80
68.	Wholesale & retail trade	5,706.43	5,228.11	-478.32	-8.38
69.	Finance & insurance	813.04	796.72	-16.32	-2.01
70.	Real estate & rental	1,260.74	1,152.40	-108.34	-8.59
71.	Hotels, personal & repair svcs.	814.35	808.05	-6.30	-0.77
72.	Business services	257.97	248.44	-9.53	-3.69
73.	Automobile repair & svcs.	234.11	229.32	-4.79	-2.05
74.	Amusement	200.23	198.30	-1.93	-0.96
75.	Medical, educ. svcs., & nonprofit org.	2,310.37	2,085.02	-225.35	-9.75
76.	Federal govt. enterprises	545.59	519.35	-26.24	-4.81
77.	State & local govt. enterprises	3,107.73	2,834.10	-273.63	-8.80
		$\Sigma =$ 88,339.50	81,931.06	-6,408.00	-7.25

NOTES

1. Commoner deals with both scientific and economic concepts. Economists reviewing the book have suggested that it should be read for its scientific content (e.g., Lekachman [112]). But one reviewer, Peter Passell, feels that no one should pay serious attention to the economic discussion or conclusions [169].
2. One method of measuring the *real* costs of air pollution abatement is to estimate the volume of resources needed to produce a constant bill of goods, with and without pollution abatement procedures. For a regional study using this approach, see Miernyk and Sears [156].
3. The 82-order version, published in the *Survey of Current Business* (February 1974), modified as indicated in the text. Since the exercise discussed here is purely *illustrative*, I have made no attempt to repeat the analysis with more recent data [217].
4. This involved using the 367-order table to shift electrical utilities from sector 68 in the 82-order table to the energy sector, as defined in the text.
5. I realize that auto emissions contribute heavily to pollution. The conclusions in this chapter should apply to transportation, as well as to stationary sources, but limitations of time and data precluded investigation of this sector. For a discussion of the effects of conservation policies on the use of energy in transporation, see Hirst [96].
6. Pollution coefficients, *p*, were calculated for each sector by the relation $p = (e_{ij} \cdot P)/X_i$, where e_{ij} = the energy row coefficient, P = total pollution emissions from energy sources, and X_i = total gross output in each processing sector.
7. The ten sectors, and their sector numbers as given in the tables at the end of this chapter, are: (7) energy; (13) food and kindred products; (26) chemicals and selected chemical products; (30) petroleum refining and related industries; (36) primary iron and steel manufacturing; (67) gas, water, and sanitary services; (68) wholesale and retail trade; (70) real estate and rental services; (75) medical, educational, and nonprofit organizations; and (77) state and local government enterprises.
8. See, for example, Leonard [113].
9. He says nothing about the pursuit of power and prestige—the first and second derivatives of wealth—but it would take us too far afield to discuss those matters here.

PART III

Regional Economics and Regional Science: Some Unconventional Views

Chapter 7

Bioeconomics: Interregional
and International Implications

BIOECONOMICS

It is too early to tell whether bioeconomics should be regarded as a new hybrid discipline, or more modestly as a new paradigm in the evolution of economic thought.[1] Whichever it is, bioeconomics makes a distinct break with the past. It is without doubt the most revolutionary approach to economic analysis in the history of the discipline. Other economic paradigms—including the Keynesian "revolution" and Leontief's input–output model—have distinct historical roots. As new and different as the Keynesian and input–output models are, they fit smoothly into the evolution of economic thought. As far as I have been able to determine, there are no historical antecedents for the *system of thought* called bioeconomics, although its founder does not claim to be the first to use the term.

The undisputed father of bioeconomics is Nicholas Georgescu-Roegen, and the fundamentals of this new paradigm—or new discipline, if that is how one wishes to view it—are given in his 1971 classic, *The Entropy Law and the Economic Process* [71]. Georgescu has since elaborated and refined his original ideas in a series of articles, some of which have been reprinted in *Energy and Economic Myths: Institutional and Analytical Essays* [70]. The most concise and nontechnical description of the fundamentals are given in his brief article "A Bioeconomic Viewpoint" [66].

A central tenet of all traditional systems of economic thought is the need for "continuous" economic growth.[2] Since perpetual growth in a finite environment is a logical absurdity, traditional economists agree that growth will, of course, end some day.[3] But the end of growth in traditional models is always beyond an ever-receding horizon. The appeal of perpetual economic growth is easily understood. Traditional economists are unwilling to contemplate the "unthinkable" alternative of a world in which the majority of people would be condemned to a subsistence standard of living, or even less, a world of slow or zero economic growth. This is particularly true of economists in the United States. While honoring Georgescu-Roegen for earlier achievements, the economics "establishment" has stubbornly ignored the development of bioeconomics.[4] Traditional economists have continued to insist that the only acceptable "solution" to contemporary economic problems' is an increased growth rate.

Georgescu-Roegen rejects the mechanistic basis of traditional economic theory.[5] Instead of continuous growth, Georgescu-Roegen substitutes a life-cycle model of the economic process. It could be illustrated by the standard graph that depicts a one-variable production function—including the range of *absolutely* diminishing returns—if time is substituted for the variable input on the horizontal axis. That would be a good "working approximation" of the bioeconomic process because diminishing returns is essentially what it is about.

Georgescu-Roegen's analytical foundation is, or course, far more complex. It is based on the second law of thermodynamics—the entropy law. He has used the simple device of an hourglass to illustrate the continuous, and *irreversible*, transformation of energy from its *free* or available form into *bound* or unavailable energy [74]. But the entropic process is not limited to energy; it applies also to resources, or to "matter" in its most general form [72, 73, 74].

The basic proposition of bioeconomics is that the effects of economic growth on the economic system are *cumulative and irreversible*. There is much more to his analytical system than this proposition. But it is the essential and revolutionary core of Georgescu's new approach to economic analysis, and the only one that will be elaborated in this chapter.

The idea of economic decline is not by itself a revolutionary proposition—certainly not in regional economics or regional science. Once the spatial dimension is explicitly taken into account, many regional concerns revolve around economic decline, as well as economic growth, especially when policy issues are being considered. Historically, the

Table 7–1. **Annual Growth Rates in GNP Per Employed Worker,
1963–1979**

Country	Growth Rates	
	1963–73	*1973–79*
United States	1.9%	0.1%
Japan	8.7	3.4
West Germany	4.6	3.2
France	4.6	2.7
United Kingdom	3.0	0.3
Italy	5.4	1.6
Canada	2.4	0.4

Source: Economic Report of the President [208], p. 85.

coexistence of growing and declining regions has been regarded as an entirely "normal consequence" of evolutionary change. But since the beginning of the era of growth—which coincides roughly with the Industrial Revolution—such regional changes have taken place in the context of *national* economic growth, defined as rising real income per capita. The influence of national growth on regional theorizing has been strong. Much regional theory has been concerned, in one way or another, with the geographical distribution of national economic growth.[6] But national economic growth rates have dropped sharply during the past decade. Table 7–1 shows that this has been true not only in the United States but also in other industrialized countries.

Many economists appear to view the slow growth of the seventies as a temporary phenomenon induced by political rather than economic events. Lester Thurow's book, *The Zero Sum Society* [206], typifies the thinking of many conventional economists. Stagflation, and everything that awkward neologism implies, are the products of political ineptitude. The nation's economic problems could be solved, Thurow maintains, by more intelligent political behavior. We have the economic tools, he believes, to solve our economic problems—even to the extent of becoming energy independent—if we only had the political will and skill to do so.

A bioeconomic interpretation of the events Thurow discusses is quite different. Without questioning Thurow's hypothesis that political leaders are inept, it brings in a powerful influence that he and other traditional economists have ignored, namely, the growing worldwide scarcities of matter and energy. Slow growth, declining productivity, inflation—all the problems, in brief, that have so thoroughly frustrated conventional economists—have their roots in the growing scarcity of *mattergy*, to use a felicitous word coined by Kenneth Boulding in an unpublished poem. There is no doubt that these problems have been exacerbated by the political process, with its frequently contradictory policies. But even an ideal political system would not "solve" the scarcity problem, once the centerpiece of economic analysis, but now largely superseded by the specious doctrine of "unlimited substitutability."[7]

Those who accept the doctrine of unlimited substitutability with equanimity have no difficulty with its natural corollary of unlimited growth, or at least unlimited growth in the "foreseeable future." The latter term is sufficiently extensile to serve as a working synonym for "forever." This proclivity is reinforced by the widespread acceptance of growth models that can be described by smooth, continuously differentiable functions. It might help shake off some old habits of thought if we replace these smooth growth trends by a new model that permits sudden, discrete changes. The following section describes my attempt to make a first cut along these lines.

A CATASTROPHE THEORY OF ECONOMIC GROWTH

Catastrophe theory is one of those misnomers that crop up occasionally in the evolution of scientific thought. It is not, in the words of Poston and Stewart, "a single thread of ideas; it resembles more closely a web, with innumerable interconnected strands; these include physical intuition and experiment, geometry, algebra, calculus, topology, singularity theory, and many others. This web is itself connected to and imbedded in a larger web: the theory of dynamical systems. . ." [180, p. 7].

Catastrophe theory has been described by Zeeman as "a new mathematical method of describing the evolution of forms in nature" [229, p. 1]. Although the theory was invented by René Thom in 1972, the best explications in the English language are Zeeman's, who published a lucid and detailed description of catastrophe theory in *Scientific American* [229]. The following discussion draws heavily on that paper. (See also van Kijk and Nijkamp [223].)

As Zeeman has pointed out, catastrophe theory is "particularly applicable where gradually changing forces produce sudden effects. We often call such effects catastrophes, because our intuition about the underlying continuity of the forces makes the very discontinuity of the effects so unexpected. . ." [228, p. 1]. Many of the early examples of "elementary catastrophes," as Thom called the basic archetypal forms he had discovered, were taken from physics, although much of his original book dealt with embryology. There have been numerous applications to psychology, and some to the social sciences. But Zeeman believes that the greatest potential is probably in the field of biology. This is what suggested that some of the basic ideas of catastrophe theory could be applied to the regional aspect of bioeconomics.[8] I have used one of Thom's catastrophes to illustrate graphically the regional impacts of the transition from a growth to a no-growth economy. The geometric model is given in Figure 7–1.

Figure 7–1 describes the "cusp" catastrophe, one of the seven elementary catastrophes derived by Thom. It has two "control dimensions" (growth or no-growth), and one behavior dimension—regional income distribution in this model—described by the behavior surface.[9]

The behavior surface can be described by a sheet of paper twisted to obtain a smooth fold in the center. The "bifurcation set" is projected from the behavior surface in two dimensions in the same way that indifference curves are projected from a production surface in neoclassical theory.

The cusp model describes, in starkly simple terms, the highly complex behavior of economic actors under the two conditions postulated by the control surface. When the national economy is growing (the expansion catastrophe), there is economic growth in all regions. Under these conditions, there is slow convergence of per capita income among regions. This is partly explained by conventional theory.[10] But it is explained in part by simple arithmetic. Small absolute changes measured from a low-income base yield large relative changes, while fairly large changes from high-income bases can result in small percentage changes.

There is a shift from the expansion catastrophe to a contraction catastrophe under no-growth conditions. The behavior surface now describes a process of regional redistribution. Between points B and A there is accelerated convergence. By the time point A has been reached, the per capita income positions of some regions will have switched. Some formerly above-average regions will have dropped below the national average, and some formerly below-average regions will have risen above it.

The essential point to be made by the use of this simple model in a regional context is that under conditions of robust national growth everyone can be involved in the process of accumulation. Some regions grow more rapidly than others, but as long as all regions grow, the problem of distribution—or redistribution—is not a matter of great

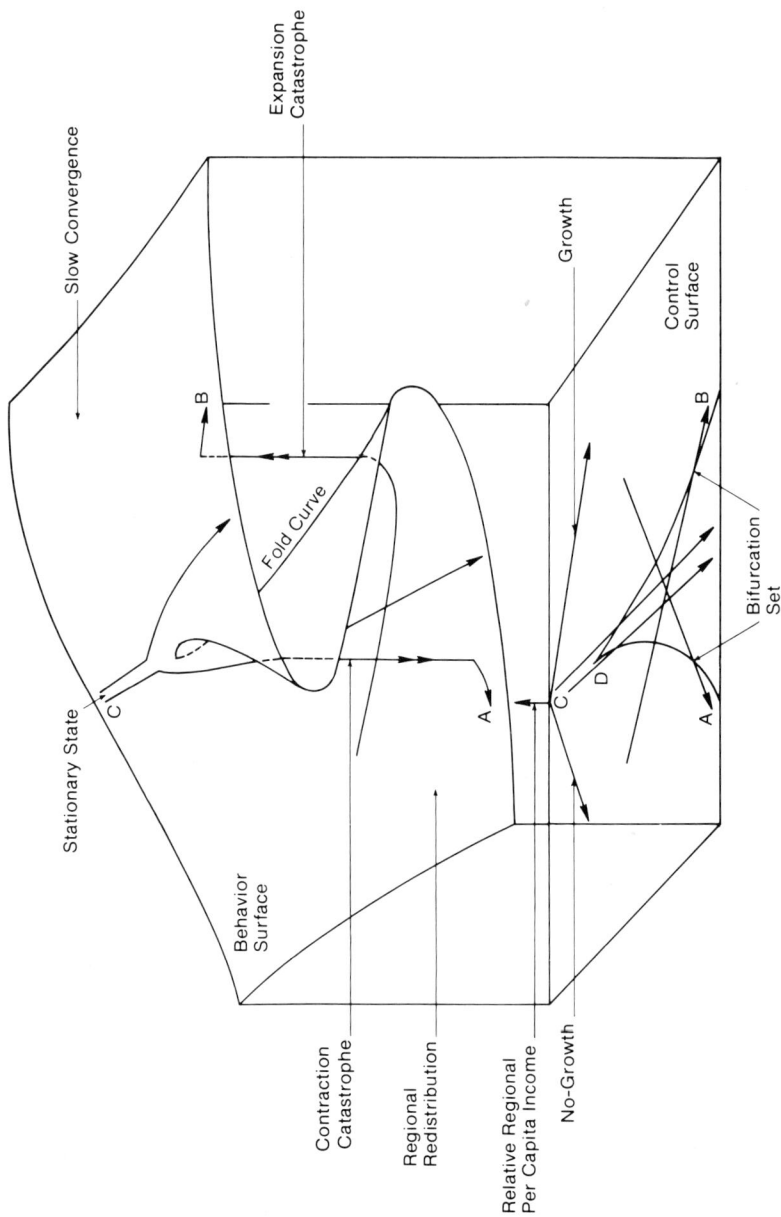

Figure 7–1. Cusp model of changes in relative regional per capita income.

Note: This is an adaptation of Zeeman's "aggression" model described in *Scientific American* [228], p. 66. Used by permission of W.H. Freeman and Company, Publishers.

concern. The end of robust national growth does not mean, as Figure 7–1 might suggest, a stationary state in "dynamic equilibrium." The stationary state represents a "neutral" point on the behavior surface. It is the cusp in two dimensions (point D in Figure 7–1).

At no time in the history of the United States has there been uniform growth among regions. Depending on how one defines "regions," concomitant growth and decline has been the normal state of affairs in a growing national economy. The end of national economic growth would not mean the end of growth for all regions. What it would mean, however, is that the economic process would become a zero-sum game; some regions would grow at the expense of others. Regional wealth and income would be redistributed.

The catastrophe model has severe analytical limitations. In Zeeman's words, Figure 7–1 describes "a phenomenological model only; it cannot yet be said to explain the behavior" described [228, p. 69]. But such a model can have heuristic value; it can lead one to search for the continuous underlying forces that are responsible for discrete changes. These forces are described in Figure 7–2.

Both world population and energy demand have been increasing exponentially since about the middle of the last century. Until the 1950s, however, the population curve lay well above the energy-demand trend. Moreover, until the late 1960s, world energy supply increased at least as rapidly as demand—at times more rapidly—so real energy prices were either stable or declining.

During the 1950s, energy demand began to rise more quickly than population, and the two curves crossed.[11] Moreover, because of growing constraints, energy supply rose more slowly than demand after the late 1960s with accompanying increases in energy prices. Over the long term, this situation is likely to continue.

Figures 7–1 and 7–2 cannot be linked directly; the former has no time dimension while the latter does. But there was a sudden drop in the U.S. economic growth rate during the 1970s, which for practical purposes can be considered a discrete change.[12] This drop is largely the result of energy supply constraints. It is not a temporary phenomenon; we'll have to live with it indefinitely.

INTERREGIONAL EFFECTS OF SLOW OR ZERO NATIONAL ECONOMIC GROWTH

Trends in relative regional per capita income, by BEA regions, are given in Figure 7–3. The data through 1977 are from the source shown; the projections are mine. The trends to 1969 can be related to

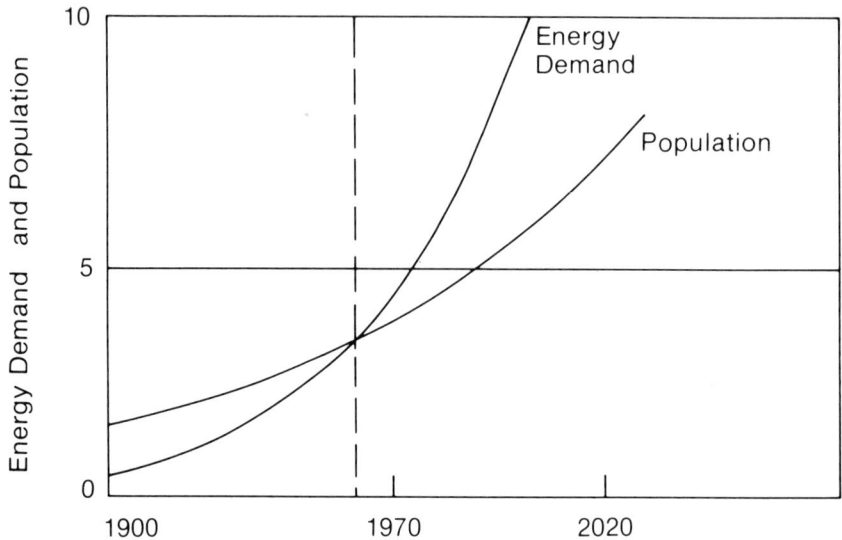

Note: Energy is expressed in billion metric tons of coal equivalent; population is in billions.

Source: "Thinking About Energy," by Barbara B. Fogel, *RF Illustrated,* April 1980; Rockefeller Foundation. Used by permission of The Rockefeller Foundation.

Figure 7–2. World energy demand and population.

the expansionist catastrophe portion of Figure 7–1. The period between 1969 and 1989 corresponds to the portion of the behavior surface between points B and A. And the projections after 1989 relate to the "regional redistribution" portion of the behavior surface.

Like the catastrophe model, Figure 7–3 explains nothing; it has to be explained. The explanation I offer is that growing supply constraints—on both matter and energy—are changing old patterns of development. The standard development model (still accepted by the World Bank, among others) is described in its simplest outlines by the solid lines of Figure 7–4. It shows the relationship between the structure of production and GNP per capita generally associated with the names of Colin Clark and A. G. B. Fisher.[13]

This chart is cross-sectional; it shows that countries heavily dependent on primary activities (agriculture, forestry, and fishing) have low GNP per capita, while those primarily devoted to tertiary activities (trades, services, research, and development, for example) have high GNP per capita. But Clark and Fisher found the same relationships over time as individual countries went through the process of struc-

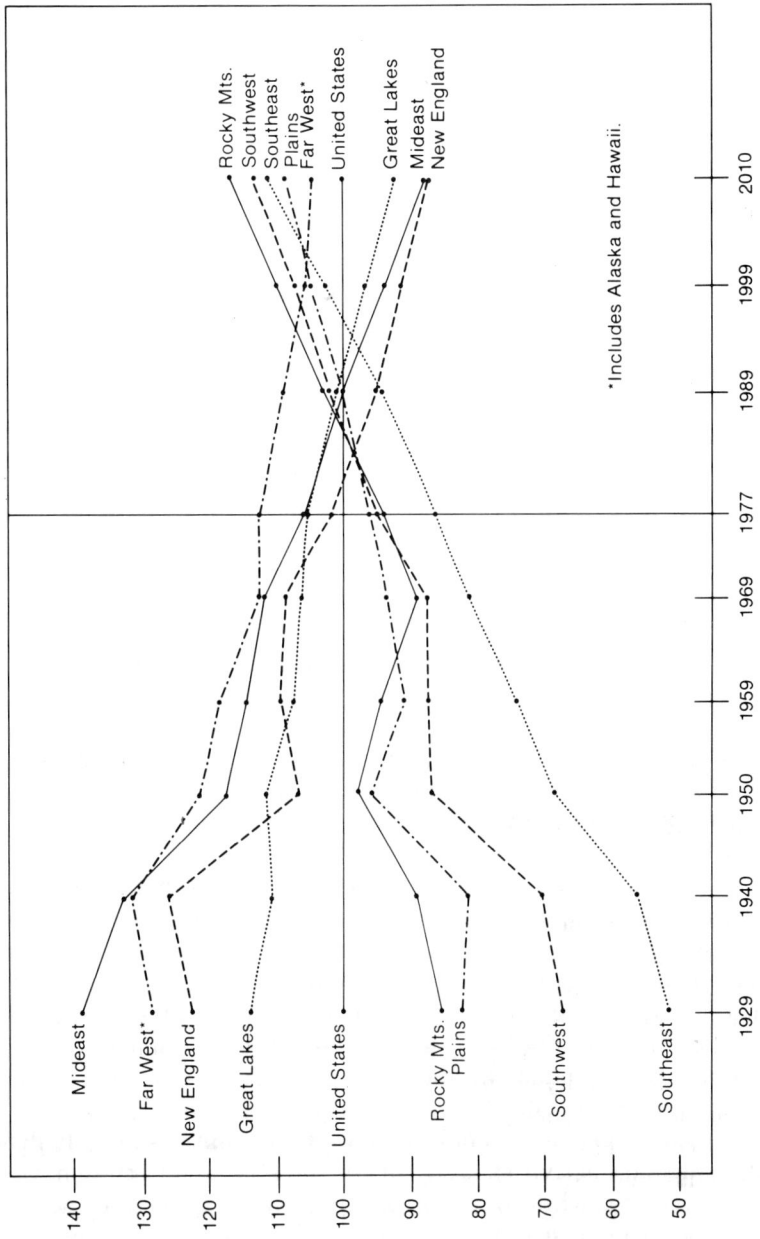

Figure 7–3. **Trends in relative regional per capita income.**

Source: 1929–1977, U.S. Department of Commerce, Bureau of Economic Analysis, *Survey of Current Business* (October 1978), p. 27.

*Includes Alaska and Hawaii.

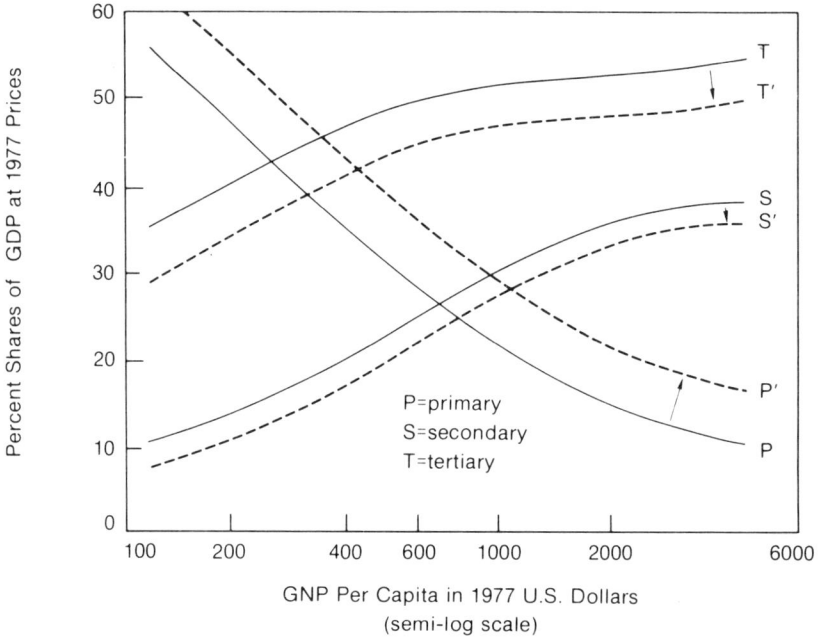

Source: Solid lines, *World Development Report, 1979.* New York: Oxford University Press (August 1979), p. 44, used by permission. Dotted lines, author's projections.

Figure 7–4. Transformation of production.

tural transformation we refer to loosely as "economic development." Louis Bean, among others, also found this relationship among regions in the United States [13].

There is evidence, however, that the Clark–Fisher–Bean relationship was breaking down in this country during the 1970s.[14] There is no reason to believe the U.S. experience is unique. Indeed, a recent study by Kader suggests it is not [104].

Dependence on primary activities, and the extractive parts of the secondary sector (i.e., gas, oil, and mining), are no longer low-wage, low-price activities. Energy-producing states have been among those with the most rapidly rising per capita incomes; states entirely dependent on imported energy have experienced relative declines in per capita income. This accounts for much of the accelerated convergence in regional per capita incomes after 1969 shown in Figure 7–3.[15] Windfall gains from oil decontrol are likely to accelerate the process of convergence [97, p. 91].

The dashed lines in Figure 7–4 summarize the short-term effects of structural transformation. Regions producing energy and primary products will enjoy increasing shares of gross domestic product, as well as rising GNP per capita. There will be offsetting declines in energy-importing manufacturing regions, and those highly specialized in tertiary activities. As pointed out elsewhere [155], this is largely a result of shifting terms of trade.

Data to support this contention are scanty, but some examples will illustrate the point. In 1949–50, a year's tuition at Harvard College cost $1,305. A West Virginia coal operator wishing to send his son to Harvard would have had to sell 249.5 tons of coal, at the prevailing average price of $5.23 per ton, to pay his son's expenses. Harvard has done an excellent job of keeping up with inflation. By 1979–80, a year's tuition at Harvard College cost $8,330. But a West Virginia coal operator would have had to sell only 238 tons of coal, at $35 per ton, to pay this expense. The shift in the terms of trade here has been slight. Nevertheless, it has been in favor of the coal operator.

Another example shows a much sharper shift in the terms of trade. In 1950, a West Virginia coal operator would have had to pay $208.70 for a year's premium on a $10,000 John Hancock life insurance policy. He would have had to sell 40 tons of coal, at $5.23 per ton, to make this payment. By 1980, because of the effects of inflation on the yields of insurance company investments, the premium had dropped to $163.30. If the coal operator had bought a $10,000 policy that year, he would have had to sell only 4.7 tons at $35 per ton to pay a year's premium. It's more likely, of course, that because of inflation he would have bought a $50,000 policy, which would have cost $825.50. But he still would have had to sell only 23.6 tons of coal to pay the premium on the larger policy. The terms of trade have shifted drastically here.[16]

Fragmentary data to make such Ricardian comparisons of shifts in the terms of trade are hard to come by. But simple comparisons of energy price changes by state lend further support to the hypothesis that the terms of trade are turning in favor of energy-producing states.[17] The evidence is not as clear-cut in the case of agricultural states because of short-term fluctuations in farm prices, but Kansas, Nebraska, and Iowa, which historically have had relatively low per capita incomes, are now close to or above the U.S. average.

POLICY IMPLICATIONS

When a national economy enjoys robust growth, as did the U.S. economy, say, between 1960 and 1965, many economic problems are mitigated. This is a good time for lagging regions to try to catch up with those that have traditionally or historically enjoyed above-average levels of real per capita income. It is under such conditions that national programs to stimulate economic development in lagging regions can be initiated. In this country we have the examples of the Area Redevelopment Administration, the Appalachian Regional Commission, and the Economic Development Administration (discussed in Part II). The objectives of all three programs were similar: to identify the causes of slow growth in those areas. The greatest demand for such assistance came from representatives of the "depressed" areas. But the representatives of wealthier regions either supported redevelopment efforts or at least did not oppose them.

The situation can change dramatically, however, when the national growth rate falls rapidly. It soon becomes evident that all regions are not getting larger shares of an ever-growing pie, but that output and incomes in some regions are rising rapidly at the expense of other regions. This situation, unless it is approached with understanding based on dispassionate analysis, could lead to a virulent form of sectionalism which is the antithesis of a regionalist approach to national—indeed, global—problems.[18]

INTERNATIONAL IMPLICATIONS

The title of this chapter is somewhat misleading since it gives equal billing to the international and interregional implications of the basic principles of bioeconomics. But no attempt was made to replicate the interregional analysis at the international level. The international problem is a logical extension of the interregional problem, but it will be far more serious and prove to be much more intractable. Interregional income differentials within the United States are almost negligible compared to those between the "developed" and "less developed" nations of the world. Scattered indicators show some redistribution of real income, but it has been—by and large—from oil-importing countries to the members of OPEC [208, pp. 168–169]. Other indicators show some modest shift in real income from North America to Western Europe and Asia (most likely to Japan), but virtually no shift to the less developed countries [165].

CONCLUSIONS

Part of this chapter has been built around a simple, topological model that is completely devoid of explanatory power. The model is further burdened, in my opinion, by an unfortunate name. But it has the useful property of describing how a set of phenomena that can be expressed in terms of continuous functions can produce another phenomenon that represents a discrete change.

Let me stress that the use of this model is not intended to revive the Malthusian spectre, nor to forecast a Meadows-type cataclysm. When a particular region or nation reaches the point represented by the cusp in Figure 7–1, economic growth will end, but actual changes will occur far more gradually than those depicted by this simple model.[19]

On the other hand, the conclusions of the analysis discussed here are completely at variance with those of futurists and technological optimists who believe that for some reason, which they do not explain, we are presently going through a difficult "transition" that ultimately will lead to high and rising per capita income for the world's steadily growing population.[20]

The concept of *limited* substitutability is not only valid, it is essential to any meaningful dynamic analysis. But there is no scientific basis for the hypothesis of "unlimited substitutability," or for the belief that we will be able to discover unlimited quantities of renewable energy that could provide rising per capita incomes for the 8 billion people who will inhabit the globe at the turn of the century. This is only wishful thinking at its worst. There is a scientific basis for the assumption that the second law of thermodynamics will continue to hold, and that the economic problem of the future will be one of meeting the basic needs of a growing population with a steadily dwindling—and thus increasingly scarce—stock of energy and resources.

If Georgescu-Roegen's bioeconomic principles are true—and they have not been successfully challenged on either logical or empirical grounds—we will have to recognize that the classical economists were right. The economic process is, and always has been, one of allocating *scarce* resources. Even if there is positive economic growth for decades, there will not be enough for all regions in all industrialized countries to grow. It is even less likely that all nations *can* grow.

The process of interregional and international redistribution will continue. The rate at which the process will go on—and whether it will be accomplished peacefully, or increasingly by various kinds of military, terroristic, or economic warfare—are matters one can only speculate about at this time. If economics is to be rescued from its present state of disarray, however, economists will have to turn to the principles of bioeconomics and stop looking for a technological *deus ex machina* to usher in the Age of Abundance, which never really had a chance of making it on this side of Alice's looking glass.

NOTES

1. The term "paradigm" is used here as defined by Kuhn [110, pp. 176–177].
2. As used here, the terms "traditional" or "conventional" economics include the neoclassical, Keynesian, post-Keynesian, and Marxist systems.
3. For a lucid and convincing demonstration of the inevitable end of economic growth—and the unwillingness of most segments of society to accept this fact—see Bartlett [12].
4. This has not been true in Europe, however. See, for example, Georgescu-Roegen [67] and Zamagni [227]. It would also be wrong to suggest that Georgescu's new doctrine has had no impact on the thinking of American economists. For a highly favorable review of *Energy and Economic Myths*, see Canterbery [29].
5. An illustration of the mechanistic nature of conventional economics is given by the standard circular flow diagram found in virtually all elementary economic texts. These diagrams are supposed to represent the economic process by showing the flow of goods and services in one direction with offsetting flows of money (in the broadest sense of that term) in the other. What they show, however, is perpetual motion since there is nothing in the model to suggest that either of the flows alter the economic system in any way.
6. See, for example, Richardson [187, 188]; Borts and Stein [22]; von Böventer [224, 225]; and Miernyk [149].
7. See Goeller and Weinberg [79].
8. For other applications of catastrophe theory to regional issues, see van Kijk and Nijkamp [223] and Wilson [226].
9. The control surface is defined by the parameters a and b in a potential function of the form $\frac{1}{4}x^4 - ax - \frac{1}{2}bx^2$. The parameters represent "bundles" of opposing forces; a is the bundle of forces retarding growth, while b is the bundle of forces stimulating growth. For each pair of parameters defining the control surface, there is a corresponding variable x representing relative regional per capita income. The behavior surface is generated by all the points obtained when the first derivative of the potential function is set equal to zero, i.e., when $x^3 - a - bx = 0$. For a more detailed discussion of the cusp catastrophe, related to a different set of economic considerations, see van Kijk and Nijkamp [223].
10. The best concise description of this process is given by Borts and Stein [23].
11. The projections to 2020 are Fogel's, given in Figure 7–2. The energy demand projection assumes "low economic growth and moderate conservation." She also assumes that energy supply will increase at an even faster rate. I disagree with both projections, but agree that the demand trend will continue to rise faster than the population trend.
12. Between 1963 and 1973 the "doubling time" of GNP per employed worker was about 35 years. Since 1973 it has stretched to 700 years.
13. The source from which Figure 7–4 was taken includes a similar diagram showing the relationship between the structure of employment and GNP per population. The pattern is almost identical with that of Figure 7–4. For the Clark–Fisher references, see Miernyk [135].
14. The statistical details are too lengthy to attempt to summarize here. They are given in two earlier papers [135, 152].
15. For further details, see Corrigan and Stanfield [39] and Miernyk [152].
16. I am grateful to the Office of Analytical Studies, Harvard University, and to the Research Office of John Hancock Mutual Life Insurance Company for the data used

in these illustrations. The historical coal prices are from the *Minerals Yearbook* [218]; the 1979–80 coal prices are Regional Research Institute estimates.

17. Some of these are given in Miernyk, Giarratani, and Socher [155]. A number of additional examples of shifts in the terms of trade between energy-surplus and energy-deficit states similar to those in the text are given in Miernyk [140].

18. For a discussion of the issues involved in the "Sunbelt–Snowbelt" controversy, see Rafuse [182] and *Business Week* [199]. For related discussions of regional income shifts, and some of their political repercussions, see Haveman et al. [91]; Moody and Puffer [161]; and *The Wall Street Journal* [167].

19. Although one can argue that at some hypothetical point the shift from growth to no-growth will represent a discrete change—a 180-degree turn—the change actually will be slow and gradual. Because of the complexity of the economic process, and wide disparities in personal income distribution, some individuals will continue to experience rising real incomes even after the average real income of the region has started to decline.

20. For excellent antidotes to the excesses of Utopian futurists and technological optimists, see Georgescu-Roegen [68] and Renshaw [185].

Chapter 8

The Realism and Relevance of Regional Science

THE ORIGINS OF REGIONAL SCIENCE

Regional science is the newest of the social sciences. The roots of regional economics—the precursor of regional science—can be traced to von Thüen's *Der isolierte Staat*, published in 1826. The birth of regional science as a separate discipline came much later, however. It can be dated rather precisely as December 27, 1954. This is when approximately sixty economists, geographers, planners, and others with an interest in spatial analysis met to form the Regional Science Association. The guiding light of this meeting was Walter Isard, the founder and still the prime mover of regional science.

The brief minutes of the first RSA business meeting indicate that it was far from clear that the new organization would survive. The general view appeared to be that the association should make haste slowly. Even Isard "indicated that a skeleton type of organization would be adequate for most purposes" [184]. The first volume of *Papers and Proceedings* was a mimeographed document. Some contributors to this meeting submitted only abstracts for inclusion in the *Proceedings*; they preferred to publish their complete papers elsewhere.

Twenty-two years later, regional science was firmly established as an independent discipline with a broad international base. The January 1976 *RSA Newsletter* listed nineteen regional science journals or serials and fourteen series of monographs, bibliographies, and reports. Today's regional science journals are able to attract articles that compare favorably, both methodologically and substantively, with those of other professional societies.

Courses in regional science were offered until recently only at the university where Walter Isard happened to be teaching. Initially, this was MIT. Later Isard moved to the University of Pennsylvania, where the first full-fledged Department of Regional Science was established, and then to Cornell. Isard also started the Regional Science Research Institute, which continues to function as as independent entity. The January 1976 *Newsletter* [183] reports that fourteen universities are known to offer degree programs and specializations in regional science today. In addition to those in the United States, such programs are located in Australia, Italy, Belgium, Germany, England, and Austria.

This brief recapitulation of events of the past two decades shows that regional science is now a firmly established discipline. Regional scientists know this, but most academics do not; it is known even less in the world of practical affairs.

In part, the relative anonymity of regional science is simply a reflection of the newness of the discipline. But there are other contributing factors. First is the ambiguity that continues to surround the definition of regional science. In his recent *Introduction to Regional Science*, Isard gives thirteen definitions [100, p. 5]. Without any loss of generality, however, these definitions can be synthesized into one: *Regional science is the study of those social, economic, political, and behavioral phenomena that have a spatial dimension.*[1] But can all these aspects of human behavior be handled within the confines of a single discipline? Isard has long felt that they can [101].

In some respects, Isard's vision of regional science is similar to that of Auguste Comte's vision of sociology. Comte believed that scientific thought would continue to evolve until it reached what he called "a positive stage," which would mark the end of scientific evolution. Comte grasped the notion that "knowledge in the various sciences is unified and related" [128, p. 177]. And he believed that all the strands of scientific thought would ultimately converge in a positive sociology. Comte clearly overestimated the capability of any scientist to keep abreast of developments in all fields. But he felt that at some point, perhaps in the distant future, there would be a single *unified* science.

Similarly, Isard and his followers do not regard regional science as an interdisciplinary activity; it is a new, unified discipline.

THE DUAL IDENTITY OF REGIONAL SCIENTISTS

Some members of regional science associations might question this characterization. This is because most of us who belong to regional science organizations have a dual identity. We are geographers and regional scientists; economists and regional scientists; planners and regional scientists; and so forth. Indeed, Charles Leven, whose contributions to regional science have been substantial, remarked in private conversation several years ago that at that time there was only one *true* regional scientist—Walter Isard.

The dual identity of regional scientists is easy to understand. Most of us came out of established disciplines, and most of us have spent our careers in traditional departments such as economics, city and regional planning, geography, and sociology. The early graduates of the first Ph.D. program in regional science also found employment in traditional departments. But as the number of regional science departments increases, it is likely that a growing number of regional scientists will shed their dual identity and will be known exclusively as regional scientists. This conclusion is predicated, of course, on the assumption that regional science will continue to evolve and to expand. It should continue to evolve, of course, as part of mankind's general intellectual evolution. But the rate at which the discipline will grow depends, in my view, on the extent to which future "consumers" of education and research believe that regional science is a realistic discipline, and one whose methods can be used to analyze issues of contemporary political, social, and economic concern. And this will happen, I believe, only if we and our students are able to avoid the methodological pitfalls of the other social sciences.

Since I am an economist in the other half of my dual identity, let me illustrate the point by reference to the field of economics. It is no secret that the present state of economics has been severely criticized from within by such luminaries as Leontief [118], Georgescu-Roegen [69], Galbraith [62], and Baumol [11]. A 1976 article in *Fortune* [15] illustrates a growing skepticism about the usefulness of contemporary economics as viewed from outside. Economists also have been lampooned by journalists, including Art Buchwald and Russell Baker. I suspect that the hastily written columns of the latter have more impact on the public mind than the combined lucubrations of those of us who labor in academic vineyards.

CRITIQUES OF CONTEMPORARY ECONOMICS

A quarter of a century ago, a typical issue of *The American Economic Review* would include several articles dealing with contemporary economic problems, one or two articles of a theoretical nature, and an occasional article on methodology. It was still considered proper to relegate mathematical discussion to an appendix, and while some articles included the kinds of graphs still found in intermediate textbooks, most were devoid of symbolic presentations. But Samuelson's *Foundations of Economic Analysis* had been published in 1947, and even before that he had started the stream of journal articles that only in recent years has shown any tendency toward abatement. While it might be unfair to attribute the dramatic change in the character of economic analysis that has occurred over the past quarter century to any one individual, I think few would quarrel with the statement that Samuelson's influence on modern neoclassical economics has been paramount (cf. Solo [201]). Today, a typical issue of *The American Economic Review*, or for that matter almost *any* economic journal, contains a high proportion of articles that have more to do with mathematics—complete with theorems, proofs, and lemmas—than with any recognizable economic issue. Many of those related to economic issues tend to be highly recondite, and in order to keep the mathematics tractable deal with the completely unreal world of "perfect competition."[2]

Shortly before the trend leading to the present state of economics had been firmly established, Frank Knight, in his presidential address to the American Economic Association, had been led to wonder "whether economists, and particularly theorists, may not be in the position that Cicero, citing Cato, ascribed to the augurs of Rome [the ancient Roman officials whose job it was to observe and interpret omens for the guidance of public affairs]—that they should cover their faces or burst into laughter when they met on the street" [108, p. 2]. He felt that the published work of economists "must have *some* relation to the public interest if we are to expect public support; and why they pay us for it anyway is one of the deep economic mysteries. . .of popular economic irrationality" [108, pp. 4–5]. But Knight's evaluation had no apparent impact on subsequent events. His presidential address came at a time when most of the published work of economists dealt with problems and issues of contemporary concern. One cannot help wondering, however, if Knight did not have a clear intuition of what was to come.

A far more devastating methodological attack was leveled by Wassily Leontief, who received the 1973 Nobel Prize in Economics, in his presidential address. Leontief criticized the pretentious mathematical models that had come to dominate the pages of economic journals by the time he spoke. His qualms about these models were not caused by "the *irrelevance* of the practical problems to which present day economists address their efforts, but rather by the palpable *inadequacy* of the scientific means with which they try to solve them" [118, p. 1]. "A typical theoretical model," he continued, "can be handled now as a routine assembly job. All principle components. . .come in several standard types; so does the optional equipment. . . ." Much of the discussion of these models consists of a "step-by-step derivation of its formal properties." The accuracy of these mathematical manipulations can generally be taken for granted. "Nevertheless, they are usually spelled out at great length. By the time it comes to interpretation of the substantive *conclusions*, the assumptions on which the model has been based are easily forgotten. But it is precisely the empirical validity of these *assumptions* on which the usefulness of the entire exercise depends" [118, p. 2].

Leontief objects to the lack of realism in much of contemporary economics. He is not attacking the use of mathematics *per se* in economics. Indeed, anyone familiar with Leontief's writings is aware that he is an accomplished mathematician, and that his earlier publications in particular contain a great deal of involved mathematics. But to him mathematics has been a tool used to reach an analytical objective, rather than an end in itself.

In the early 1950s, when a growing number of journal articles were liberally sprinkled with equations, derivations, and proofs, some economists questioned the legitimacy of the application of rigorous analytical techniques to a discipline whose data consisted of relatively mushy estimates. Defenders of the new methodological approach pointed out that it has certain advantages. Properly done, it forces the analyst to write out his assumptions explicitly, and to carry through his analysis with logical rigor. By contrast, a purely verbal analysis can be bogged down in a semantic morass. Anyone who has waded through the voluminous growth pole–growth center literature will agree that this danger exists (see Darwent [47]). Thus the issue is not whether mathematics should or should not be used as an analytical tool. The issue is whether it will be used as a tool or—to use a felicitous term suggested by Heller [94]—largely for "recreational purposes."

Baumol, another economist with impeccable mathematical credentials, has commented on this: "Elaborate superstructures are erected to show off spectacular applications of esoteric theorems with little regard for relevance or illumination. The writer indulges himself in what has been described by a great economist as illicit intercourse with beautiful models" [11, p. 93].

In his 1974 presidential address to the AEA, Walter Heller sought to redress what he considered to be an unbalanced view of the present state of economics. In the first section of his address, he performed a useful function by succinctly summarizing the critical views of Galbraith, Leontief, and Boulding. He also summarized the criticisms made by other distinguished economists in their presidential addresses to a number of associations, including the Econometric Society, Section F of the British Association, the Royal Economics Society, the Southern Economic Association, the American Finance Association, and the Eastern Economic Association. Most of his discussion, however, is devoted to an attempt to show "what's right with economics"—the title of his address.

Heller feels that "many competent, tough, and rigorously trained minds have been drawn into economics in response not just to challenging policy problems but to the quantitative revolution since World War II" [94, p. 4]. These economists, he goes on to tell us, "can draw on a hard core of economic theory and methodology, together with a growing body of empirical knowledge, to provide standards for testing the validity (*though not necessarily the relevance and reality*) of ideas, analysis, and empirical findings" (emphasis added). Heller tried to convince his listeners not only that modern economics has made major advances on the methodological and analytical fronts, but that it has become a highly useful discipline. I find his effort totally unconvincing. He mentions, of course, the successful 1964 tax cut as one instance in which the effects projected by economists correspond closely to the subsequent reality. But how long can economics continue to coast on a single successful application of a simple Keynesian model? One need not be an economist to be aware that other exercises in applied macroeconomics have not worked. Indeed, I have a feeling that one reason many economists prefer to deal with abstract exercises today is that they have nothing to say that would be even remotely interesting to those charged with the making and implementation of economic policy. And when public pronouncements are made by eminent neoclassical economists today, they often refer to such parameters as the "appropriate" rate of growth or "desirable" unemployment rates and price increases. Such pronouncements require nothing in the way of analytical backup.

The February 1976 issue of *The Quarterly Journal of Economics* is a case in point. The first thirty-seven pages is devoted to a series of tributes to the late Alvin H. Hansen by a half-dozen former students and colleagues, including Paul Samuelson and James Tobin. Most commented on the pragmatic basis of Hansen's theorizing and his lifelong preoccupation with the application of economic analysis to public policy. Above all else, Hansen was concerned with realism and relevance. To quote Samuelson: "Hansen did not regard economics as an ego trip. To him it was the fascinating study of how to improve the lot of humanity" [197, p. 31]. Most of the remainder of this issue of the journal, however, is devoted to articles of the type that unequivocally fall under the heading of "mathematical recreation."

What can be said of regional science? Is there any more concern about reality among regional scientists than there is among mainstream economists? As it turns out, much of regional science *is* economics—regional economics. Thus, *mutatis mutandis* what has been said about economics could apply to regional science, and to some extent it does.

THE METHODOLOGICAL APPROACHES
OF REGIONAL SCIENCES

It is not hard to find examples of recreational mathematics in the regional science journals, particularly in recent years. But the basic orientation of most regional science research has been rather heavily empirical. Recently, for example, I asked two of my graduate assistants to classify all the articles that have been published in *The Journal of Regional Science* to date. On the basis of combined judgments, slightly more than 6 percent of the pages of the leading regional science journal have been devoted to purely theoretical articles. Almost 42 percent reported on empirical studies. It is significant, however, that articles dealing with policy issues accounted for fewer than 5 percent of the pages. The subject matter of the remaining pages was distributed as follows: input–output analysis (3 percent), linear programming models (6 percent), interregional analyses, excluding input–output (10 percent), growth models (6 percent), central place theory and applications (15 percent), and the description or application of other analytical tools (8 percent). Let me stress that there is a subjective element involved in this classification. But it is not likely that anyone else would arrive at a significantly different distribution of the content of articles under the same headings.

It would be interesting to see a similar content analysis of other regional science journals, and of the papers and proceedings of the annual meetings of various regional science associations. One might then be able to determine whether the trend in economics is being followed in regional science with an appropriate lag. There is limited evidence that it is if one compares the contents of Volume 35 of the *RSA Papers* with Volume 1. But the kind of extreme abstraction found in most contemporary economic theory is still largely absent from the pages of regional science journals and the proceedings of regional science association meetings. There is little in regional science, for example, to compare with the branch of contemporary economic theory that deals with capital and growth (Harcourt [86]). The mathematical models used to discuss the alleged behavior of the imaginary creatures who inhabit the one-product (putty, clay, or jelly) world of capital-growth theory make even some of the more abstract regional science models look highly realistic by comparison.

I have said that much of regional science *is* economics, but does this mean that *all* of contemporary regional economics fits comfortably under the regional science rubric? I feel that it does not. One area of considerable friction is that of regional growth theory.

NEOCLASSICAL ECONOMICS AND REGIONAL SCIENCE

Some economists, notably Borts and Stein, have applied neoclassical theory to the analysis of regional growth [20, 23]. Richardson has been highly critical of the assumptions of full employment and perfect competition that are implicit in neoclassical regional models [186, p. 22]. He has developed an alternative theory of growth that emphasizes agglomeration economies and locational preferences—instead of the conventional neoclassical variables of wage and capital yield differentials. Borts feels that Richardson's model "winds up as an interesting, potentially testable, and useful synthesis of locational variables *which might strengthen the neoclassical approach!*" [21, p. 546, emphasis added]. But he does not come to grips with the fundamental conflict between neoclassical theory and regional analysis pointed out earlier by Richardson. As Lösch made clear more than two decades ago, there is a basic incompatibility between spaceless neoclassical theory and location theory [127, esp. pp. 105–130]. As soon as space is explicitly introduced into an analysis—and this happens when agglomeration and locational preferences are taken into account—the assumptions of perfect competition no longer apply. At the micro level, the only model that is consistent with spatial analysis is that of monopolistic competition. Regional scientists are able to accept this; neoclassical regional economists are not.

Another part of the turf of regional science that has been "invaded" by conventional economists, with some resulting friction, is the broad area called urban economics. As might be expected, the invaders brought along their neoclassical analytical methods to produce what is referred to as the "new urban economics" in contrast to earlier studies, which were more descriptive and policy-oriented (Mills et al. [158]; Mirrlees [160]). Once again Richardson took the offensive in a critical review of recent applications of simplified neoclassical models to complex urban problems with their explicit spatial dimensions [186, 189]. He evidently succeeded in touching a sensitive nerve, since one of the targets of his attack—Robert Solow—came back with a surprising *ad hominem* rejoinder. Part of the problem, Solow asserted, was that Richardson obviously had "never seen a *real* mathematical display!" [202, p. 267].

Regional science has little if anything to gain from attempts by mainstream economists to apply contemporary neoclassical theory to regional and urban problems. Up to the present, regional science has been more problem-oriented and issue-oriented than conventional economics. And I would argue that it has been able to do this without sacrificing rigor. Space limitations preclude extensive documentation, but let me give a few examples.

The input–output model has been a favorite of regional analysts for almost twenty years. Many early regional and interregional input–output studies were exploratory, and hence had little practical value. But in the past ten years or so an increasing number of regional models have been carefully constructed from primary data, and have been successfully used for a variety of analytical purposes (Giarratani et al. [76]; Miernyk [151]). This is one of the few analytical techniques of which R. A. Gordon could speak kindly in his recent presidential address to the American Economic Association. He feels that rigor and relevance "have been successfully blended" in input–output analysis [82, p. 3]. Increasingly, input–output models are being used extensively for state planning and other administrative purposes (Emerson [56]; Giarratani et al. [76, pp. 45–62]). Early input–output research at the regional level also led to a number of useful spinoffs, such as Isard's industrial complex analysis [100].

There is a substantial and growing body of literature dealing with regional development problems and policies, both in the United States and abroad (Hansen [84, 85]; Newman [166]). Regional development policy has not been a notable success either in the United States or in other parts of the world. But in this country it has been at least as successful as monetary, fiscal, manpower, and most international policies have been in achieving their stated objectives. The nexus between regional science and policy has been somewhat closer in Japan and Western Europe than in the United States (Konno [109]). But this is because some degree of economic planning is more widely accepted in most parts of the industrialized world than it is in this country. If, as some expect, the United States is slowly moving in the direction of indicative economic planning, the policy orientation of regional science will undoubtedly be strengthened.

In his review of Richardson's *Regional Growth Theory*, Borts was critical because "the author gives no indication that interest in regional economics in the United States has declined substantially, and has been replaced by a study of the particular social and economic pathology of urban and rural areas" [21, p. 547]. This is no doubt true; traditional economics journals probably contain a smaller proportion of regional articles than they did in the past. But this decline undoubtedly has been more than offset by the recent rapid expansion of regional science journals. Interest in regional economics—narrowly defined—might well be on the wane, but interest in regional science is clearly on the rise. Potentially, this could represent a net gain to society.

It should be obvious that I view regional science today as a more realistic discipline than the dominant branch of contemporary economics with its emphasis on neoclassical theory. It also is more relevant to current issues and problems than much of conventional economics. There is a tendency, however, for the newest of the social sciences to ape the older discipline from which it was derived. Since I agree with those who believe that modern neoclassical economics is involved in an ever-tightening spiral of trivialization, I do not regard this trend as a healthy one.

The trenchant criticisms of Knight, Leontief, Galbraith, Boulding, Georgescu-Roegen, and other giants of the profession have had little impact on contemporary economics. Their criticisms have not been answered; they have simply been ignored. Why is this so? First, as Blackman has pointed out, "The profession's incentive system tends perversely to reward this kind of endeavor and to deflect the attention of gifted economists from the exploration of concrete problems and the dirty work that entails" (see Heller [94, p. 2]). Galbraith provides part of the answer when he points out that business censorship, which was once a stultifying force in academic economics, has been replaced by a new despotism that consists of "defining scientific excellence as whatever is closest in belief and method to the scholarly tendency of the people who are already there" [62, p. 2]. As long as those who control the system of rewards and the channels of publication in economics insist on maintaining the priority of a system of belief over reality, it is likely that the drift away from realism and relevance, and toward increasing sterility, will go on. I hope that regional science will not continue its own slow drift in the same direction.

NOTES

1. This differs from an earlier synthesis that did not include the word "behavioral" [146].
2. On this, see Solo [201], especially pp. 632–633.

References

[1] Adams, F. Gerard, Carl G. Brooking, and Norman J. Glickman, "On the Specification and Simulation of a Regional Econometric Model: A Model of Mississippi," *Review of Economics and Statistics* 57 (August 1975), pp. 286–298.

[2] Adams, F. Gerard, and Norman J. Glickman (eds.), *Modeling the Multiregional Economic System*. Lexington, Mass.: Lexington Books, D. C. Heath and Company (1980).

[3] Almon, Clopper, *The American Economy to 1975: An Interindustry Forecast*. New York: Harper and Row (1966).

[4] Almon, Clopper, M. B. Buckler, L. M. Horwitz, and T. C. Reimbold, *1985: Interindustry Forecasts of the American Economy*. Lexington, Mass.: Lexington Books, D. C. Heath and Company (1974).

[5] Appalachian Regional Commission, *Appalachia—A Reference Book*, 2nd ed. Washington, D.C. (February 1977).

[6] ———, *1979 Annual Report*. Washington, D.C. (1979).

[7] Ballard, Kenneth P., et al., "A Bottom-Up Approach to Multiregional Modeling: NRIES," presented to the Conference on *Modeling the Multi-Region Economic System*, Philadelphia (June 14–15, 1979).

[8] Ballard, Kenneth P., and Norman J. Glickman, "A Multi-Regional Forecasting System: A Model for the Delaware Valley," *Journal of Regional Science* 17 (August 1977), pp. 161–177.

[9] Ballard, Kenneth P., Richard D. Gustely, and Robert M. Wendling, *NRIES: Structure, Performance, and Application of a Bottom-Up Interregional Econometric Model*. Washington, D.C.: U.S. Department of Commerce, Bureau of Economic Analysis, Regional Economic Analysis Division (March 1980).

[10] Ballard, Kenneth P., and Robert M. Wendling, "The National-Regional Impact Evaluation System: A Spatial Model of U.S. Economic and Demographic Activity," *Journal of Regional Science* 20 (May 1980), pp.143–158.

[11] Baumol, William J., "Economic Models and Mathematics," in *The Structure of Economic Science*, Sherman Roy Krupp (ed.). Englewood Cliffs, N.J.: Prentice-Hall (1966), pp. 88–101.

[12] Bartlett, Albert A., "The Forgotten Fundamentals of the Energy Crisis," *American Journal of Physics* 46 (September 1978), pp. 876–888.

[13] Bean, Louis H., "International Industrialization and Per Capita Income," Part V, *Studies in Income and Wealth*. Washington, D.C.: National Bureau of Economic Research (1946), pp. 119–143.

[14] Bell, Frederick W., "An Econometric Forecasting Model of a Region," *Journal of Regional Science* 7 (1967), pp. 109–127.

[15] Beman, Lewis, "The Chastening of the Washington Economists," *Fortune* (January 1976), pp. 158–166.

[16] Berg, Charles A., "Conservation in Industry," *Science* 184 (April 19, 1974), pp. 264–270.

[17] Beyers, William B., "On the Stability of Interregional Models: The Washington Data for 1963 and 1967," *Journal of Regional Science* 12 (December 1972), pp. 363–374.

[18] Bolton, Roger, "Multiregional Models: Introduction to a Symposium," *Journal of Regional Science* 20 (May 1980), pp. 131–142.

[19] ———, "Multiregional Models in Policy Analysis," in *Modeling the Multiregional Economic System*, F. G. Adams and N. J. Glickman (eds.). Lexington, Mass.: Lexington Books, D. C. Heath and Company (1980), pp. 255–283.

[20] Borts, George H., "Criteria for the Evaluation of Regional Development Programs," in *Regional Accounts for Policy Decisions*, Werner Z. Hirsch (ed.). Baltimore: The Johns Hopkins University Press (1966), pp. 183–218.

[21] ———, Review of *Regional Growth Theory*, by Harry W. Richardson, in *Journal of Economic Literature* 12 (June 1974), pp. 546–547.

[22] Borts, G. H., and J. L. Stein, *Economic Growth in a Free Market*. New York: Columbia University Press (1964).

[23] ———, "Regional Growth and Maturity in the United States: A Study of Regional Structural Change," *Schweizerische Zeitschrift für Volkswirtschaft und Statistik* 98 (1962), pp. 290–321.

[24] *Boston Sunday Globe*, "Do-Nothing Bureaucracy Squanders Millions of Tax Dollars" (8 October 1972).

[25] Bozdogan, Kirkor, D. Wheeler, G. DeSouza, B. Kasting, D. Menegakis, R. Nadkarni, and N. Talbot, *The Impact of National Energy and Environmental Policies on Industry Location Dynamics*. Cambridge, Mass.: Report submitted to U.S. Department of Energy, Office of Policy and Evaluation, by Arthur D. Little, Inc. (February 1979).

[26] Brown, Murray, Maurizio diPalma, and Bruno Ferrara, "A Regional-National Econometric Model of Italy," *Papers of the Regional Science Association* 29 (1972), pp. 25–44.

[27] Buckler, Margaret B., D. Gilmartin, and T. C. Reimbold, "The INFORUM Model," in *Advances in Input-Output Analysis*, Karen R. Polenske and Jiri V. Skolka (eds.). Cambridge, Mass.: Ballinger Publishing Company (1976), pp. 297–327.

[28] Cameron, G. C., "The Regional Problem in the United States—Some Reflections on a Viable Federal Strategy," *Regional Studies* 2 (1968), pp. 207–220.

[29] Canterbery, E. Ray, Review of *Energy and Economic Myths*, by Nicholas Georgescu-Roegen, in *Southern Economic Journal* 46 (October 1979), pp. 655–657.

[30] Carley, William M., "Uranium Drain: Fuel Shortage Forecast for U.S. Nuclear Plants Within A Decade or Two," *Wall Street Journal* (June 7, 1976).

[31] Cartwright, Joseph V., "Estimating the Spatial Distribution of Program Impacts Within Metropolitan Areas," U.S. Department of Commerce, Bureau of Economic Analysis, presented to the Annual Meeting, Southern Regional Science Association, Nashville (April 1979).

[32] Cartwright, Joseph V., et al., "The Regional Impact of Changes in Construction Spending: An Analysis of SMSA Multiplier Differentials." Washington, D.C.: U.S. Department of Commerce, Bureau of Economic Analysis, mimeographed (June 25, 1979).

[33] Chancellor, W. J., and J. R. Goss, "Balancing Energy and Food Production, 1975-2000," *Science* 192:4236 (April 16, 1976), pp. 213–218.

[34] Chenery, Hollis, "Regional Analysis," in *The Structure and Growth of the Italian Economy*, H. Chenery and P. Clark (eds.). Washington, D.C., U.S. Mutual Security Agency (1953), pp. 96–115.

[35] Chinitz, Benjamin, and Monroe Newman, *Title V Regional Commissions: An Evaluation*. Prepared for the Office of Regional Economic Coordination, U.S. Department of Commerce (undated).

[36] Clark, Colin, *The Conditions of Economic Progress*. London: Macmillan (1940).

[37] Commoner, Barry, *The Poverty of Power: Energy and the Economic Crisis*. New York: Alfred A. Knopf (1976).

[38] Corrigan, Richard, "An Economic War Over Oil Also Looms at the State Level," *National Journal* 51–52 (December 22, 1979), pp. 2137–2138.

[39] Corrigan, Richard, and Rochelle L. Stanfield, "Rising Energy Prices— What's Good for Some States Is Bad for Others," *National Journal* 12:12 (March 22, 1980), pp. 468–474.

[40] Courbis, Raymond, and Dominique Vallet, "An Interindustry Interregional Table of the French Economy," in *Advances in Input–Output Analysis*, Karen R. Polenske and Jiri V. Skolka (eds.). Cambridge, Mass.: Ballinger Publishing Company (1976), pp. 231–249.

[41] Crow, Robert T., "A Nationally Linked Regional Econometric Model," *Journal of Regional Science* 13 (August 1973), pp. 187–204.

[42] Cumberland, John H., *Regional Development Experiences and Prospects in the United States of America*. Paris: Mouton (1971).

[43] Czamanski, Stanislaw, *Regional Science Techniques in Practice*. Lexington, Mass.: Lexington Books, D. C. Heath and Company (1972).

[44] Daly, Herman E., "Entropy, Growth, and the Political Economy of Scarcity," in *Scarcity and Growth Reconsidered*, V. Kerry Smith (ed.). Baltimore: The Johns Hopkins University Press (1979), pp. 67–94.

[45] ——, "The Steady-State Economy: Toward a Political Economy of Biophysical Equilibrium and Moral Growth," in *Toward a Steady-State Economy*, H. E. Daly (ed.). San Francisco: W. H. Freeman and Company (1973), pp. 149–174.

[46] Danziger, Sheldon, and Robert Haveman, "Tax and Welfare Simplification: An Analysis of Distributional and Regional Impacts," *National Tax Journal* 30 (1977), pp. 269–283.

[47] Darwent, D. F., "Growth Poles and Growth Centers in Regional Planning—A Review," *Environment and Planning* 1 (1969), pp. 5–31.

[48] Denison, Edward F., *Accounting for Slower Growth: The United States in the 1970s*. Washington, D.C.: The Brookings Institution (1979).

[49] "Does Pollution Control Waste Too Much Energy?" *Business Week* (March 29, 1976), p. 72.

[50] Dowling, J. M., and F. R. Glahe (eds.), *Readings in Econometric Theory*. Boulder: Colorado Associated University Press (1970).

[51] Drake, Ronald L., "A Short-Cut to Estimates of Regional Input–Output Multipliers: Methodology and Evaluation," *International Regional Science Review* 1 (Fall 1976), pp. 1–17.

[52] Dresch, Stephan P., and Robert D. Goldberg, "IDIOM," *Annals of Economic and Social Measurement* 2 (1973), pp. 232–356.

[53] Dresch, Stephan P., and Robert A. Updegrove, *IDIOM: Current Status and Direction of Development*. New Haven, Conn.: Institute for Demographic and Economic Studies (July 1977).

[54] Dutta, M., and V. Su, "An Econometric Model of Puerto Rico," *Review of Economic Studies* 36 (July 1969), pp. 319–333.

[55] Emerson, M. Jarvin, "Interregional Trade Effects in Static and Dynamic Input-Output Models," in *Advances in Input–Output Analysis*, Karen R. Polenske and Jiri V. Skolka (eds.). Cambridge, Mass.: Ballinger Publishing Company (1976), pp. 263–278.

[56] ———, "Large Scale Models in Regional Development Planning," *Regional Science Perspectives* 4 (1974), pp. 1–17.

[57] Fisher, Allan G. B., *The Clash of Progress and Security*. New York: Sentry Press (1966).

[58] Fisher, Anthony C., and Frederick M. Peterson, "The Environment in Economics: A Survey," *Journal of Economic Literature* 14:1 (March 1976), pp. 1–33.

[59] Fishkind, Henry H., "The Regional Impact of Monetary Policy: An Economic Study of Indiana," *Journal of Regional Science* 17 (1977), pp. 77–88.

[60] Fleming, Marcus, "External Economies and the Doctrine of Balanced Growth," *The Economic Journal* 65 (June 1955), pp. 241–256.

[61] Funck, Rolf, and Gerhard Rembald, "A Multi-Region, Multi-Sector Forecasting Model for the Federal Republic of Germany," *Papers of the Regional Science Association* 34 (1975), pp. 69–82.

[62] Galbraith, J. K., "Power and the Useful Economist," *The American Economic Review* 63 (March 1963), pp. 1–11.

[63] Garnick, Daniel H., "A Reappraisal of the Outlook for Northern Cities in the Context of U.S. Economic History," presented to the Second Annual Conference on the Economic Future of the Northeast States, MIT–Harvard (January 25, 1978).

[64] Garnick, Daniel, and Vernon Renshaw, "Competing Hypotheses on the Outlook for Cities and Regions: What the Data Reveal and Conceal," *Papers of the Regional Science Association* 45 (November 1979), pp. 105–124.

[65] Garnsey, Morris E., *American New Frontier*. New York: Alfred A. Knopf (1950).

[66] Georgescu-Roegen, Nicholas, "A Bioeconomic Viewpoint," *Review of Social Economy* 35:3 (December 1977), pp. 361–375.

[67] ———, *Demain la Décroissance*, translated with a preface by Ivo Rens and Jacques Grinevald. Paris: Pierre-Marcel Favre (1979).

[68] ———, "Energy Analysis and Economic Valuation," *Southern Economic Journal* 45:4 (April 1979), pp. 1023–1058.

[69] ———, "Energy and Economic Myths," *The Southern Economic Journal* 41 (January 1975), pp. 347–381.

[70] ———, *Energy and Economic Myths: Institutional and Analytical Essays*. New York: Pergamon Press (1976).

[71] ———, *The Entropy Law and the Economic Process*. Cambridge, Mass.: Harvard University Press (1971).

[72] ———, "Matter: A Resource Ignored by Thermodynamics," in *Proceedings of the World Conference on Future Sources of Organic Materials*. Toronto (July 10–13, 1978).

[73] ———, "Matter Matters Too," in *Prospects for Growth: Changing Expectations for the Future*, K. D. Wilson (ed.). New York: Praeger (1977).

[74] ———, "Myths About Energy and Matter," *Growth and Change* 10:1 (January 1979), pp. 16–22.

[75] ———, "The Steady-State and Ecological Salvation: A Thermodynamic Analysis," *Bioscience* 27:4 (April 1977), pp. 266–269.

[76] Giarratani, Frank, James Maddy, and Charles F. Socher, *Regional and Interregional Input–Output Analysis: An Annotated Bibliography*. Morgantown: West Virginia University Library (1976).

[77] Glickman, Norman J., *Econometric Analysis of Regional Systems*. New York: Academic Press (1977).

[78] ———, "An Econometric Forecasting Model for the Philadelphia Region," *Journal of Regional Science* 11 (1971), pp. 15–32.

[79] Goeller, H. E., and Alvin M. Weinberg, "The Age of Substitutability," *The American Economic Review* 68:6 (December 1978), pp. 1–11.

[80] Golladay, Frederick, and Robert Haveman, *The Economic Impacts of Tax-Transfer Policy: Regional and Distributional Effects*. New York: Academic Press (1977).

[81] ———, "Regional Distributional Effects of a Negative Income Tax," *The American Economic Review* 65 (1976), pp. 629–641.

[82] Gordon, Robert Aaron, "Rigor and Relevance in a Changing Institutional Setting," *The American Economic Review* 66 (March 1976), pp. 1–14.

[83] Hall, Owen P., and Joseph A. Licari, "Building Small Region Econometric Models: Extension of Glickman's Structure to Los Angeles," *Journal of Regional Science* 14 (1974), pp. 337–353.

[84] Hansen, Niles M., *Public Policy and Regional Economic Development*, Cambridge, Mass.: Ballinger Publishing Company (1974).

[85] ———, *Rural Poverty and the Urban Crisis*. Bloomington: Indiana University Press (1970).

[86] Harcourt, G. C., "Some Cambridge Controversies in the Theory of Capital," *Journal of Economic Literature* 7 (June 1969), pp. 369–405.

[87] Harris, Curtis C., Jr., "A Multiregional, Multi-Industry Forecasting Model," *Papers of the Regional Science Association* 25 (1970), pp. 169–180.

[88] ———, "New Developments and Extensions of the Multiregional-Multiforecasting Model," *Journal of Regional Science* 20 (May 1980), pp. 159–172.

[89] Harris, Curtis C., Jr., and Frank E. Hopkins, *Locational Analysis: An Interregional Econometric Model of Agriculture, Mining, Manufacturing, and Services.* Lexington, Mass.: Lexington Books, D. C. Heath and Company (1972).

[90] Haveman, Robert H., "Evaluating the Impact of Public Policies on Regional Welfare," *Regional Studies* 10 (1976), pp. 449–463.

[91] Haveman, J., R. L. Stanfield, and N. R. Peirce, "Federal Spending: The North's Loss Is the Sunbelt's Gain," *National Journal* 26 (June 26, 1976), pp. 878–891.

[92] Haveman, Robert H., et al., "The Poverty Institute Regional and Distributional Model—Its Application to the Program for Better Jobs and Income," mimeographed (1978).

[93] Hayes, Dennis, "Conservation as a Major Energy Source: Efficiency and Insulation Offer Savings on Fuel," *The New York Times* (March 21, 1976).

[94] Heller, Walter W., "What's Right with Economics?" *The American Economic Review* 65 (March 1975), pp. 1–26.

[95] Hirschman, Albert O., "Industrial Development in the Brazilian Northeast and the Tax Credit Scheme of Article 34/18," *The Journal of Development Studies* 5:1 (October 1968), pp. 5–28.

[96] Hirst, Eric, "Transportation Energy Conservation Policies: Higher Gasoline Taxes and New Car Fuel Economy Standards Are Effective Energy Saving Policies," *Science* 192:4234 (April 2, 1976), pp. 15–20.

[97] "How Sudden Oil Wealth Is Splitting the States," *Business Week* (May 12, 1980), p. 91.

[98] Hughes, William R., "National and Regional Energy Models," *Growth and Change* 10 (January 1979), pp. 92–103. "Comment," by Gary J. Koehler, p. 104.

[99] Isard, Walter, "Interregional and Regional Input-Output Analysis: A Model of the Space Economy," *The Review of Economics and Statistics* 33 (1951), pp. 318–328.

[100] ———, *Introduction to Regional Science.* Englewood Cliffs, N.J.: Prentice-Hall (1975).

[101] ———, *Location and Space Economy.* New York: John Wiley & Sons (1956).

[102] Isserman, Andrew M., "Estimating Export Activity in a Regional Economy: A Theoretical and Empirical Analysis of Alternative Methods," *International Regional Science Review* 5 (Winter 1980), pp. 155–184.

[103] Johnston, J., *Econometric Methods*, 2nd ed. New York: McGraw-Hill (1972).

[104] Kader, Ahmad A., "Primary Oriented Countries and Changes in Economic Structure," *Atlantic Economic Journal* 9:1 (March 1981), pp. 90–91.

[105] Kahn, Herman, William Brown, and Leon Martel, *The Next 200 Years: A Scenario for America and the World*. New York: William Morrow and Company (1976).

[106] Kane, Edward J., *Economic Statistics and Econometrics*. New York: Harper & Row (1968).

[107] Keynes, John Maynard, "Economic Possibilities for Our Grandchildren," in *Essays in Persuasion*. New York: W. W. Norton and Company (1963), pp. 358–373.

[108] Knight, Frank H., "The Role of Principles in Economics and Politics," *The American Economic Review* 24 (March 1951), pp. 1–29.

[109] Konno, Genpachiro, "Prospects and Tasks of Regional Science in Developing Countries," *Papers of the Regional Science Association* (November 1974), pp. 7–22.

[110] Kuhn, Thomas S., *The Structure of Scientific Revolutions*, 2nd ed. Chicago: The University of Chicago Press (1970).

[111] Latham, William R., Kenneth A. Lewis, and John H. Landon, "Regional Econometric Models: Specification and Simulation of a Quarterly Alternative for Small Regions," *Journal of Regional Science* 19 (1979), pp. 1–13.

[112] Lekachman, Robert, Review of *The Poverty of Power: Energy and The Economic Crisis*, by Barry Commoner, in *The Washington Post Book World* (May 9, 1976).

[113] Leonard, William N., "In Search of an Energy Policy," *Challenge* 19:2 (May/June 1976), pp. 52–68.

[114] Leontief, Wassily, "Environmental Repercussions and the Economic Structure: An Input–Output Approach," *The Review of Economics and Statistics* 52:3 (August 1970), pp. 262–270.

[115] ———, "Interregional Theory," in *Studies in the Structure of the American Economy*, W. Leontief et al. (eds.). New York: Oxford University Press (1953), pp. 93–115.

[116] ——— (written in collaboration with Alan Strout), "Multiregional Input-Output Analysis," in *Structural Interdependence and Economic Development*, Tibor Barna (ed.). London: Macmillan (1963). Reprinted in Leontief, *Input–Output Analysis*, New York: Oxford University Press (1966).

[117] ———, "National Income, Economic Structure, and Environmental Externalities," in Milton Moss (ed.), *The Measurement of Economic and Social Performance*. New York: National Bureau of Economic Research (1973), pp. 565–576.

[118] ———, "Theoretical Assumptions and Nonobserved Facts," *The American Economic Review* 61 (March 1971), pp. 1–7.

[119] Leontief, Wassily, and Daniel Ford, "Air Pollution and the Economic Structure: Empirical Results of Input-Output Computations," in *Input–*

Output Techniques, A. Brody and A. P. Carter (eds.). Amsterdam: North-Holland Publishing Company (1972), pp. 9–30.

[120] Leontief, Wassily, A. Morgan, K. R. Polenske, D. Simpson, and E. Tower, "The Economic Impact—Industrial and Regional—of an Arms Cut," *The Review of Economics and Statistics* (August 1965), pp. 217–241.

[121] L'Esperance, W. L., *The Structure and Control of a State Economy*. London: Pion Ltd. (1981).

[122] L'Esperance, W. L., A. E. King, and R. H. Sines, "Conjoining an Ohio Input–Output Model with an Econometric Model of Ohio," *Regional Science Perspectives* 7 (1977), pp. 54–77.

[123] L'Esperance, W. L., G. Nestel, and D. Fromm, "Gross State Product and an Econometric Model of a State," *Journal of the American Statistical Association* 64 (September 1969), pp. 787–807.

[124] Levitan, Sar A., *Federal Aid to Depressed Areas*, Baltimore: The Johns Hopkins University Press (1964).

[125] Liebenberg, Maurice, Albert A. Hirsch, and Joel Popkin, "A Quarterly Econometric Model of the United States," *Survey of Current Business* 46 (May 1966), pp. 13–39.

[126] Lincoln, G. A., "Energy Conservation: Some Challenges Are Proposed for Science and Technology," *Science* 180:4082 (April 13, 1973), pp. 155–180.

[127] Lösch, August, *The Economics of Location*. New Haven, Conn.: Yale University Press (1954).

[128] Mazlish, Bruce, "Auguste Comte," in *The Encyclopedia of Philosophy*, Vol. 2. New York: Macmillan and the Free Press (1967), pp. 173–177.

[129] Miernyk, William H., Review of *Advances in Input-Output Analysis*, by Karen R. Polenske and Jiri V. Skolka (eds.), in *Journal of Regional Science* 18 (August 1978), pp. 313–316.

[130] ———, "Appalachia: The Revival of a Depressed Regional Economy," presented to the International Symposium on the Ruhr Area, sponsored by the Konrad Adenauer Institute, Essen, Federal Republic of Germany (May 4, 1979).

[131] ———, "Area Redevelopment," in *In Aid of the Unemployed*, J. M. Becker (ed.). Baltimore: The Johns Hopkins University Press (1966), pp. 158–171.

[132] ———, "Bioeconomics: Interregional and International Implications," presented to the First World Regional Science Congress, Cambridge, Mass. (June 11, 1980), revised version.

[133] ———, "British and American Approaches to Structural Unemployment," *Industrial and Labor Relations Review* 12:1 (October 1958), pp. 3–19.

[134] ———, "British Regional Development Policy," *Journal of Economic Issues* 3:3 (April 1970), pp. 27–32.

[135] ———, "The Changing Structure of the Southern Economy," in *The Economics of Southern Growth*, E. Blaine Liner and Lawrence K. Lynch

(eds.). Research Triangle Park, N.C.: The Southern Growth Policies Board (1977).

[136] ———, "Coal," in *Collective Bargaining: Contemporary American Experience*, Gerald G. Somers (ed.). Madison, Wis.: Industrial Relations Research Association (1980).

[137] ———, "Comments on Recent Developments in Regional Input–Output Analysis," *International Regional Science Review* 1 (Fall 1976), pp. 47–55.

[138] ———, "Decline of the Northern Perimeter," *Society* (May/June 1976), pp. 24–26.

[139] ———, *Depressed Industrial Areas—A National Problem*, Planning Pamphlet No. 98. Washington, D.C.: National Planning Association (January 1957).

[140] ———, "The Differential Effects of Rising Energy Prices on Regional Income and Employment," presented to the RFF/Brookings Conference, Washington, D.C. (October 9–10, 1980).

[141] ———, "EDA and the Objectives of Regional Development Policy," *Explorations in Economic Research* 4:3 (Summer 1977), pp. 390–408.

[142] ———, "An Evaluation: The Tools of Regional Development Policy," *Growth and Change* 11:2 (April 1980), pp. 2–6.

[143] ———, "Experience Under the British Local Employment Acts of 1960 and 1963," *Industrial and Labor Relations Review* 20:1 (October 1966), pp. 30–49. Comment by A. P. Thirlwall with a Reply by W. H. Miernyk, *idem.* 20:4 (July 1967), pp. 667–671.

[144] ———, "An Interindustry Forecasting Model with Water Quantity and Quality Constraints," in *Proceedings, Fourth Symposium on Water Resource Research*. Ohio State University, Water Resources Center (1970), pp. 49–58.

[145] ———, "International and Multiregional Models: An Overview and Appraisal," in K. Bozdogan et al. (eds.), *The Impact of National Energy and Environmental Policies on Industry Location Dynamics*. Cambridge, Mass.: Report submitted to the U.S. Department of Energy, Office of Policy and Evaluation, by Arthur D. Little, Inc. (February 1979).

[146] ———, Review of *Introduction to Regional Science*, by Walter Isard, *Growth and Change* (April 1976), pp. 59–60.

[147] ———, "Jobs and Income," in *Appalachian Conference on Balanced Growth and Economic Development*. Washington, D.C.: Appalachian Regional Commission (October 1977).

[148] ———, "Local Labor Market Effects of New Plant Locations," in *Essays in Regional Economics*, John F. Kain and John Meyer (eds.). Cambridge, Mass.: Harvard University Press (1971), pp. 161–185.

[149] ———, "A Note on Recent Regional Growth Theories," *The Journal of Regional Science* 19:3 (August 1979), pp. 303–308.

[150] ———, "The Projection of Technical Coefficients for Medium-Term Forecasting," in *Medium-Term Dynamic Forecasting*, W. F. Gossling (ed.). London: Input–Output Publishing Company (1975), pp. 29–41.

[151] ——, "Regional and Interregional Input-Output Models: A Reappraisal," in *Spatial, Regional and Population Economics*, Mark Perlman, Charles Leven, and Benjamin Chinitz (eds.). London: Gordon and Breach, Science Publishers, Ltd. (1973), pp. 263–292.

[152] ——, "Regional Shifts in Economic Base and Structure in the United States Since 1940," in *Alternatives to Confrontation: A National Policy Toward Regional Change*, Victor L. Arnold (ed.). Lexington, Mass.: Lexington Books, D. C. Heath and Company (1980).

[153] ——, "Resource Constraints and Regional Development Policy," *Atlantic Economic Journal* 8:3 (September 1979), pp. 16–24.

[154] ——, "Simulazione di sviluppo regionale con un modello input-out," *Revista Internazionale di Scienze Economiche e Commerciali* 16 (1967), pp. 741–753.

[155] Miernyk, William H., Frank Giarratani, and Charles F. Socher, *Regional Impacts of Rising Energy Prices*, Cambridge, Mass.: Ballinger Publishing Company (1978).

[156] Miernyk, William H. and John T. Sears, *Air Pollution Abatement and Regional Economic Development*, Lexington, Mass.: Lexington Books, D. C. Heath and Company (1974).

[157] Miernyk, William H., Kenneth L. Shellhammer, Ronald L. Coccari, Wesley H. Wineman, Charles J. Gallagher, and Douglas M. Brown, *Simulating Regional Economic Development*, Lexington, Mass.: Lexington Books, D. C. Heath and Company (1970).

[158] Mills, E. S., J. MacKinnon, R. M. Solow, Y. Oron, D. Pines, E. Sheshinski, and A. Dixit, "Symposium on the New Urban Economics," *The Bell Journal of Economics and Management Science* 4 (Autumn 1973), pp. 593–651.

[159] Milne, William J., Norman J. Glickman, and F. Gerard Adams, "A Framework for Analyzing Regional Growth and Decline: A Multiregion Econometric Model of the United States," *Journal of Regional Science* 20 (May 1980), pp. 173–190.

[160] Mirrlees, J. A., "Rejoinder to Richardson—II," *Urban Studies* 10 (1973), pp. 267–269.

[161] Moody, Harold T., and Frank W. Puffer, "A Gross Regional Product Approach to Regional Model Building," *Western Economic Journal* 7 (1969), pp. 391–402.

[162] The Morgan Guaranty Trust Company, *Morgan Guaranty Survey* (February 1978), p. 8.

[163] Moses, Leon, "A General Equilibrium Model of Production, Interregional Trade and Location of Industry," *The Review of Economics and Statistics* 42 (November 1960), pp. 373–397.

[164] Moynihan, Daniel P., "The Politics and Economics of Regional Growth," *The Public Interest* 51 (Spring 1978), pp. 3–21.

[165] *The New York Times* (December 30, 1979), Section 12, p. 2.

[166] Newman, Monroe, *The Political Economy of Appalachia*, Lexington, Mass.: Lexington Books, D. C. Heath and Company (1972).

[167] "Northern States Start Drive for Federal Aid for Slack Economies," *The Wall Street Journal* (January 17, 1977).

[168] Olsen, R. J., G. W. Westley, H. W. Herzog, Jr., C. R. Kerley, D. J. Bjornstad, D. P. Vogt, L. G. Bray, S. T. Grady, and R. A. Nakosteen, *MULTIREGION: A Simulation Forecasting Model of BEA Economic Area Population and Employment.* Oak Ridge, Tenn.: Oak Ridge National Laboratory (October 1977). ORNL/RUS-25.

[169] Passell, Peter, Review of *The Poverty of Power: Energy and the Economic Crisis*, by Barry Commoner, in *The New York Times Book Review* (May 23, 1976.

[170] Peck, A. E., and O. C. Doering III, "Voluntarism and Price Response Consumer Reaction to the Energy Shortage," *The Bell Journal of Economics* 7:1 (Spring 1976), pp. 287–292.

[171] Peirce, Neil R., "Offing the Frost Belt: A Stupid Idea Whose Time Has Come," *Washington Post* (January 18, 1981).

[172] Pleeter, Saul (ed.), *Economic Impact Analysis: Methodology and Applications.* Amsterdam: Martinus Nijhoff (1980).

[173] Polenske, Karen R., "Empirical Implementation of a Multiregional Input-Output Gravity Trade Model," in *Contributions to Input–Output Analysis*, A. P. Carter and A. Brody (eds.). Amsterdam: North-Holland Publishing Company (1969), pp. 143–162.

[174] ———, "The Implementation of a Multiregional Input–Output Model of the United States," in *Input-Output Techniques*, A. Brody and A. P. Carter (eds.). Amsterdam: North-Holland Publishing Company (1972), pp. 171–189.

[175] ———, "Multiregional Interactions Between Energy and Transportation," in *Advances in Input–Output Analysis*, Karen R. Polenske and Jiri V. Skolka (eds.). Cambridge, Mass.: Ballinger Publishing Company (1976).

[176] ———, "Regional Planning and Mathematical Models," presented to the Society of Government Economists and the Econometric Society, Atlantic City, N.J. (1976).

[177] ———, *State Estimates of Technology, 1963.* Lexington, Mass.: Lexington Books, D. C. Heath and Company (1974).

[178] ———, *The U.S. Multiregional Input–Output Accounts and Model*, Lexington, Mass.: Lexington Books, D. C. Heath and Company (1980).

[179] Polenske, Karen R., et al., *State Estimates of the Gross National Product, 1947, 1958, 1963*, edited by Karen R. Polenske. Lexington, Mass.: Lexington Books, D. C. Heath and Company (1972).

[180] Poston, Tim, and Ian Stewart, *Catastrophe Theory and Its Implications.* London: Pitman (1978).

[181] Pressman, Jeffrey L., and Aaron D. Wildavsky, *Implementation.* Berkeley: University of California Press, 1973.

[182] Rafuse, Robert A., Jr., *The New Regional Debate: A National Overview.* National Governors Conference, Center for Policy Research and Analysis, Washington, D.C. (April 1977).

[183] Regional Science Association, *Newsletter* (January 1976).

[184] ———, *Papers and Proceedings*, Vol. 1 (1955).

[185] Renshaw, Edward F., *The End of Progress: Adjusting to a No-Growth Economy*. North Scituate, Mass.: Duxbury Press (1976).

[186] Richardson, Harry W., "A Comment on Some Uses of Mathematical Models in Urban Economics," *Urban Studies* 10 (1973), pp. 259–266.

[187] ———, *Regional Growth Theory*. London: Macmillan (1973).

[188] ———, "Regional Growth Theory: A Reply to von Böventer," *Urban Studies* 12 (February 1975), pp. 31–35.

[189] ———, "Reply to Solow and Mirrlees," *Urban Studies* 10 (1973), pp. 269–270.

[190] Reifler, Roger F., and Charles M. Tiebout, "Interregional Input–Output: An Empirical California–Washington Model," *Journal of Regional Science* 10 (August 1970), pp. 135–152.

[191] Roberts, Merrill, *Transportation Economics*. Universities-National Bureau Committee for Economic Research, Report of National Bureau of Economic Research. New York: Columbia University Press (1965).

[192] Rodgers, John M., *State Estimates of Interregional Commodity Trade, 1963*. Lexington, Mass.: Lexington Books, D. C. Heath and Company (1973).

[193] ———, *State Estimates of Outputs, Employment, and Payrolls, 1947, 1958, 1963*. Lexington, Mass.: Lexington Books, D. C. Heath and Company (1972).

[194] Rones, Philip L., "Moving to the Sun: Regional Job Growth, 1968–1978," *Monthly Labor Review* 103:3 (March 1980), pp. 12–19.

[195] Roy, Rustum, "Energy Education," *Science Education News* (May 1974), pp. 1–2.

[196] ———, "Plutonium and Christian Ethics," *Science* 192:4241 (May 21, 1976), pp. 738, 740.

[197] Samuelson, Paul A., "Hansen as a Creative Economic Theorist," *Quarterly Journal of Economics* 90 (February 1976), pp. 24–31.

[198] Schumacher, E. F., *Small Is Beautiful: Economics as if People Mattered*, New York: Harper & Row (1975).

[199] "The Second War Between the States," *Business Week* (May 17, 1976), pp. 92–114.

[200] Sheppach, Raymond C., *1970 and 1980 State Projections of the Gross National Product*. Lexington, Mass.: Lexington Books, D. C. Heath and Company (1972).

[201] Solo, Robert A., "Neoclassical Economics in Perspective," *Journal of Economic Issues* 9 (December 1975), pp. 627–644.

[202] Solow, Robert, "Rejoinder to Richardson—II," *Urban Studies* 10 (1973), p. 267.

[203] Stobaugh, Robert, and Daniel Yergin (eds.), *Energy Future*. New York: Random House (1979).

[204] Stone, Richard, "Whittling Away at the Residual: Some Thoughts on Denison's Growth Accounting, A Review Article," *The Journal of Economic Literature* 18:4 (December 1980), pp. 1539–1543.

[205] Thompson, Phyllis T., and John MacTavish, "Energy Conservation and Credibility," *Science* 192:4246 (June 25, 1976), p. 1286.

[206] Thurow, Lester, *The Zero Sum Society*. New York: Basic Books (1980).

[207] Treyz, George I., "Design of a Multiregional Policy Analysis Model," *Journal of Regional Science* 20 (May 1980), pp. 191–206.

[208] U.S. Council of Economic Advisers, *Economic Report of the President, January 1980*. Washington, D.C.: U.S. Government Printing Office (1980).

[209] U.S. Congress, House of Representatives, *Economic Development Programs*, Committee Print 92-17. Washington, D.C.: U.S. Government Printing Office (December 1971).

[210] ———, *Economic Development Programs*, Committee Print 93-50. Washington, D.C.: U.S. Government Printing Office (December 1974).

[211] ———, "Energy-Materials Conservation Education Act of 1975," H. R. 1708 (January 20, 1975).

[212] U.S. Congress, House of Representatives, Committee on Public Works, *Highlights of the Public Works and Economic Development Act of 1965*, 89th Cong., 1st Sess., September 1965, Committee Print No. 16. Washington, D.C.: U.S. Government Printing Office (1965).

[213] U.S. Department of Commerce, Bureau of the Census, *Statistical Abstract of the United States, 1977*. Washington, D.C.: U.S. Government Printing Office (1977).

[214] ———, *Status*. Washington, D.C.: U.S. Government Printing Office (July 1976).

[215] U.S. Department of Commerce, Bureau of Economic Analysis, Regional Economic Analysis Division, *Industry-Specific Gross Output Multipliers for BEA Economic Areas*, Guideline 5—Regional Multipliers. Washington, D.C.: U.S. Government Printing Office (January 1977).

[216] ———, "Regional and State Projections of Income, Employment, and Population to the Year 2000," *Survey of Current Business* 60:11 (November 1980), pp. 44–70.

[217] U.S. Department of Commerce, Bureau of Economic Analysis, Interindustry Economics Division, "The Input–Output Structure of the U.S. Economy: 1967," *Survey of Current Business* 54:2 (February 1974), pp. 24–56.

[218] U.S. Department of the Interior, Bureau of Mines, *1951 Minerals Yearbook*. Washington, D.C.: U.S. Government Printing Office (1952).

[219] ———, *1975 Minerals Yearbook*, Vol. I. Washington, D.C.: U.S. Government Printing Office (1977).

[220] U.S. Joint Economic Committee, "JEC Energy Subcommittee Explores Means to Reduce our Energy Consumption," *Notes from the Joint Economic Committee* 11:10 (May 14, 1976).

[221] United States Office of the Federal Register, National Archives and Records Services, *United States Government Manual 1978/79*, Appendix D. Washington, D.C.: U.S. Government Printing Office (1979).

[222] U.S. President, Office of the White House Press Secretary, "Shared Responsibility for Growth and Development," The President's Message

to Congress on His Recommendations and Findings on the White House Conference on Balanced National Growth and Economic Development. Washington, D.C. (January 19, 1979).

[223] van Kijk, Frans, and Peter Nijkamp, "Analysis of Conflicts in Dynamical Environmental Systems Via Catastrophe Theory," *Regional Science and Urban Economics* 10 (1980), pp. 429–451.

[224] von Böventer, Edwin, "Regional Growth Theory," *Urban Studies* 12 (February 1975), pp. 1–29.

[225] ———, *Theorie des Räumlichen Gleichgewichts.* Tübingen, West Germany: J. B. C. Mohr (1962).

[226] Wilson, A. G., "Aspects of Catastrophe Theory and Bifurcation Theory in Regional Science," *Papers of the Regional Science Association* 44 (1980), pp. 109–118.

[227] Zamagni, Stefano, *Georgescu-Roegen, i Fondamenti Della Teoria del Consumatore.* Milan, Italy: Estas Libri (1979).

[228] Zeeman, E. C., "Catastrophe Theory," *Scientific American* 234:4 (April 1976), pp. 65–84.

[229] ———, *Catastrophe Theory: Selected Papers 1972–1977.* Reading, Mass.: Addison-Wesley (1977).

Index

About the Author

William H. Miernyk received the B.A. degree from the University of Colorado, Boulder, in 1946, and the M.A. and Ph.D. degrees from Harvard University in 1953. He is Benedum Professor of Economics, College of Mineral and Energy Resources, and Director, Regional Research Institute, West Virginia University, Morgantown. He has taught at Northeastern University and the University of Colorado, and he has served as Visiting Professor of Economics at the Massachusetts Institute of Technology and at Harvard. He has served as consultant to the U.S. Senate Committee on Commerce and the Special Committee on Unemployment Problems, the Appalachian Regional Commission, and on advisory committees in the Commerce and Labor departments. In addition, Miernyk has been a consultant to, among others, The Brookings Institution, A. D. Little, Inc., the Battelle Institute, and CONSAD. He is the author or coauthor of numerous books, chapters in books, monographs, articles, and reviews; his most recent book, which he coauthored, is *Regional Impacts of Rising Energy Prices* (1978). Miernyk also writes a weekly column on economic issues for the *Charleston Gazette*.